Routledge Revivals

The Morality of Politics

The Morality of Politics addresses the issues of politics and morality. The book asks the questions, has politics got a moral basis? Has morality anything to do with politics? Comprised of a collection of unique essays, the book looks at the idea that politics shies away from the discussing the morality of actions and confronts evasion by clarifying some of the basic moral problems of political life. It is a unique collection in which academics holding different political and philosophical views have come together to examine some of the burning and topical issues of contemporary society. The book will appeal to all interested in the contemporary political environment and especially students of politics and moral and political philosophy.

The Morality of Politics

Bhikhu Parekh and R.N. Berki

First published in 1972
by George Allen & Unwin Ltd

This edition first published in 2018 by Routledge
2 Park Square, Milton Park, Abingdon, Oxon, OX14 4RN
and by Routledge
711 Third Avenue, New York, NY 10017

Routledge is an imprint of the Taylor & Francis Group, an informa business

© 1972 George Allen & Unwin Ltd.

All rights reserved. No part of this book may be reprinted or reproduced or utilised in any form or by any electronic, mechanical, or other means, now known or hereafter invented, including photocopying and recording, or in any information storage or retrieval system, without permission in writing from the publishers.

Publisher's Note
The publisher has gone to great lengths to ensure the quality of this reprint but points out that some imperfections in the original copies may be apparent.

Disclaimer
The publisher has made every effort to trace copyright holders and welcomes correspondence from those they have been unable to contact.

A Library of Congress record exists under LCCN: 72188882

ISBN 13: 978-0-8153-5271-6 (hbk)
ISBN 13: 978-1-351-13828-4 (ebk)
ISBN 13: 978-0-8153-5274-7 (pbk)

THE MORALITY OF POLITICS

Edited by
Bhikhu Parekh and R. N. Berki

London · George Allen & Unwin Ltd
Ruskin House Museum Street

First published in 1972

This book is copyright under the Berne Convention. All rights are reserved. Apart from any fair dealing for the purpose of private study, research, criticism or review, as permitted under the Copyright Act, 1956, no part of this publication may be reproduced, stored in a retrieval system, or transmitted, in any form or by any means, electronic, electrical, chemical, mechanical, optical, photocopying recording or otherwise, without the prior permission of the copyright owner. Enquiries should be addressed to the publishers.

© George Allen & Unwin Ltd, 1972

ISBN 0 04 320077 x hardback
    0 04 320078 8 paperback

INTRODUCTION

Has politics a moral basis? Has morality, to put it more pointedly, anything at all to do with politics? At one time, not so long ago perhaps, the question itself would have sounded absurd, and one could expect confident and almost unanimous answers in the affirmative, both from moral philosophers and from the man in the street. Today, however, there would be some doubts. It is enough to take only a fleeting glance at some of the features of political life in our age to become concerned (if not to despair) at the apparent lack of moral considerations in political life.

The immorality or amorality of politics – is there a distinction here? – would today seem to manifest itself in four principal ways. There is, first, the spectacle of inhumanity. Nothing, perhaps, characterizes better the state of politics and political morality in the contemporary world than the blandness with which some time ago the South Vietnamese government released pictures showing the torture and summary execution of Vietcong prisoners. In the old days at least, this kind of conduct, though often indulged in, was not considered something suitable to boast about. Systematic, deliberate acts of torture and cruelty to human beings, of course, are not confined to Vietnam. They are there in Latin America, in Greece, in South Africa, to mention but a few outstanding examples. The burning and maiming of innocent women and children are considered a part of 'politics', an accepted method of applying pressure on recalcitrant governments and populations, in many parts of the world, such as the Middle East.

Then, secondly, there is the phenomenon of universal selfishness. Never entirely absent from the social and political scene, today an almost exclusive concern with private and individual gains has become one of the most enduring political fetishes, especially in advanced industrial society. The standard of living has been elevated to the status of the highest moral and political value. In a world-wide context, the effects of this need no detailed documentation. The poverty, disease, and starvation of millions are facts apparently easily coexisting with the frenzied pursuit of material prosperity in the more affluent reaches of human society. Colour television sets and luxury caravans have priority over even the morsels that people might be asked to spend on foreign aid. In the domestic politics of most countries the same philosophy of narrow selfishness dominates, with consequences less conspicuous but just as disturbing. Here the placing of individual or sectional self-interest before the common good, before the public interest of the whole community, is so universal and rampant that, instead of offering moral leadership, even autocratic governments feel compelled to pander to it.

Thirdly, we can identify the phenomenon of indifference, which is at bottom the negative counterpart of inhumanity and selfishness. People look on, often literally, while human beings are killed, tortured or maltreated the world over. Their lack of compassion and commitment, their lack of a moral consciousness, their fear for their own lives and comforts above everything else, render acts of cruelty and manifestations of crass selfishness possible and profitable. Indifference can take many forms. It is there, most painfully perhaps, in the self-engineered abdication of philosophers, intellectuals, and social and political scientists in the face of evil, and their refusal to comment seriously and substantively on the morality of politics. It is there in the acquiescence of 'silent majorities' in the reappearance of a subtle kind of authoritarianism in modern society. It is there also in the blank stare and blank minds of those 'drop-outs' whose disillusionment with the prevalent immorality has led merely to the construction of phantasy worlds.

Fourth and last, we encounter the phenomenon of fanaticism and intolerance. Legitimate dissatisfaction with the way societies are run has only too easily turned into the senseless and destructive violence by the plastic-bomb throwers and rooftop snipers – these unhappy products of the civilized twentieth century. And their fanaticism is matched by an intensification of communal violence, against those having a different colour, speaking another language, or professing another religion – again to be found at such disparate places as the hills of Kashmir, the play-grounds of Alabama and the grey dwelling-houses of Belfast.

It would not be an exaggeration to conclude from all this (only a random selection of facts) that we are today living through an acute moral crisis and in particular through an agonizing state of interregnum in the morality of politics. At the very least – and nobody could say that this is all that is wanted – the facts of political life call for a thorough re-examination of the problems of political morality, for a renewed and persistent questioning of the relevant but hitherto neglected principles of moral and political philosophy.

There are hosts of questions that we urgently need to ask. Concerning inhumanity: can the deliberate causing of suffering to human beings be tolerated? Do we still hold human life sacred, a value in itself? Concerning selfishness: what does it mean to be a member of a community? Have we a moral obligation to pursue the public interest at the expense of our own? Concerning indifference: how far does moral obligation in politics extend? Does it originate in individual acts of consent, or does it stem from an underlying moral duty towards all human beings, living and unborn? Does moral obligation stop at individual doorsteps or national frontiers? Can we comment on the facts of political life without committing ourselves either in favour of or against the observance of moral principles? Concerning fanaticism and intolerance: do ends justify means in politics? Have we an obligation to try to change society, change it perhaps radically, in accordance with moral principles? Is a fully moral society possible? And if not, can we still be moral while recognizing the enduring limits of political action? These are only a handful of the problems in the broad field of political morality that require urgent consideration.

These questions are of course not new, and there is hardly a major political philosopher, from Plato to Marx, who has not tried seriously to grapple with them, and answer them in his own way. While modern society is too different from the ones familiar to these thinkers to allow straightforward adaptation of their ideas, there is much in their writings that illuminates the contemporary scene. And what we can gain from them above all is a conviction, an attitude of mind, that human problems are amenable to human control, that the establishment of a just and humane society is a possible and worth-while undertaking, that while we can never pretend to the possession of absolute knowledge, we are not reduced to a state of total scepticism. The long line of historical events that led in the twentieth century to the slow erosion of this conviction is too depressing and well known a story to need retelling here.

Against this background it is instructive to note the response of modern moral philosophy to the events that threaten to blast the very foundation of our civilization. This response, to focus our attention now on the short time-span between the First World War and the present time, has been mainly of two kinds. On the one hand, a flight into *dogmatism*, a panic-stricken stampede into the cosy world of self-styled absolute truths, infallible ideologies, the once discarded formulations of old and primitive religions. Dogmatism in morals, to give it its due, is a humanly understandable attitude, and no one can blame the man in the street, the bewildered and ignorant citizen confronted with the mass destruction of wars and revolutions, the evils of Fascism and Stalinism, the hatred, prejudice and complacency enveloping his existence from all sides, if he searches for comfort in the warmth and security of dogma. There are exonerating circumstances even in the case of philosophers and intellectuals who have sought and found refuge in this corner.

However, dogmatism must still be considered an abdication, a retrograde step leading away from heights once conquered by the philosophers of the past. A dogmatic certainty in the indisputable goodness of some moral and political values is only a poor substitute for moral philosophy. The believer might *feel* that human beings ought to be accepted as ends in themselves, that the good of the whole comprises more than the individual gains of its members, that one has an obligation to help others to live a fully human life, that a socialist (or any other) revolution will bring about a world free of injustice and inhumanity. However, in that his certainty is based merely on intuition or on the blindly accepted authority of prophetic moral teachers, the dogmatist cannot *argue* for his beliefs, cannot hope to convince others of the rightness of his moral principles or prescriptions for right conduct. Thus dogmatism fails as a response to the crisis in political morality.

On the other hand, alongside of and in a curious way reinforcing the dogmatic attitude, there has been the response of *subjectivism*. In this context, subjectivism stands for the view that moral principles are articulations of subjective emotion, and that deliberations regarding the morally most desirable way of organizing human relations in society are like acts of choosing between various brands of ice-cream. It is expressed in the once very widespread (and today still extant) conviction, shared by numerous leading intellectuals and perhaps the majority of academic moral philosophers throughout the Western world, that not only are talking morals and talking *about* morals analytically separate activities – which is true – but also that no attempt should be made to integrate them – which is patently false. An orthodoxy, especially in the Anglo-Saxon world, has grown up which looks upon the task of moral philosophy in the narrowest possible terms, confining it to the detailed investigation of 'usage' and the meanings of words encountered in moral discourse.

This is no place to go into detailed, technical criticisms of such sacred cows of contemporary moral philosophy as the 'is-ought' distinction or the doctrine of 'value-free' social science – obviously, there are more and less deserving arguments to be found on both sides in this controversy – but one can with some confidence pronounce judgement on the *impact* this kind of subjectivism has had on the state of moral consciousness in society. Dogmatism is assertive, positive and moral in its intuitive certainties, but it throws philosophy overboard. Subjectivism is rational and philosophical in its own way, but it fails to deal with problems of morality proper. Its influence, alas, spreading from the cool heights of the centres of academic learning down to the more heated atmosphere of the market-place, has tended to reinforce the attitude of indifference. This in turn has led at times to acquiescence in acts of inhumanity.

Decay, of course, cannot go on for ever, and lately there have been numerous signs indicating that thinking men are now becoming aware of the enormity of the problems facing our society and are consequently bracing themselves to the task of re-examining the morality of politics in a more satisfactory way. The long reign of logical positivism seems to be over, and 'metaphysics', once contemptuously rejected, is steadily creeping back into a state of respectability. Moral and political philosophy is awakening from its slumber, and its practitioners are once again assuming the traditional responsibilities of the man of letters. The old truth, that in order to be pertinent and interesting moral philosophy has at least to *attempt* to say something about its subject-matter proper, is gaining acceptance in ever-widening and hitherto indifferent circles. (Note, for example, the tone of Mr. G. J. Warnock's *Contemporary Moral Philosophy*, Professor Plamenatz's Introduction to his *Man and Society*, and the significant shift of emphasis between the first and the second series of Messrs Laslett and Runciman's *Philosophy, Politics and Society*.)

These signs, however, are as yet few and scattered and can easily be lost sight of in a continuing torrent of dogmatism and subjectivism. As a matter of fact, it is an interesting development in recent years that the relative weakening of the subjectivist attitude has been accompanied not only by a resurgence in the serious academic quest for illumination in the field of morals, but also by a fresh wave of dogmatism, noticeable on both sides of the Atlantic. Academic concern and commitment, to be sure, are welcome steps in the right direction, and they appear especially refreshing after the long period of drought characterizing past decades. However, this renewed academic concern with the morality of politics has sometimes gained expression in sermonizing and moralizing, in adolescent impatience and unctuous, starry-eyed romanticism (for example, many writers on the radical Right and the New Left).

Clearly, this is not what is wanted. The need is not for indignant denunciations and unilateral ideological credos, but for patient – even plodding and pedestrian – academic attempts designed slowly to disentangle the knots, and to generate a new spirit of inquiry. Big questions don't always require big answers, and it is better to start dealing with big problems in a small way rather than jump impatiently in at the deep end and get drowned in the whirling waters of one's own emotional and existential involvement. The morality of politics is a serious matter, which, indeed, *can* be left to moral and political philosophers, but only if moral and political philosophers preserve their sobriety even in their solicitude, synthesizing their dual role of citizen and academic observer.

Passionate concern for the good of humanity must be blended with the realism born of a habit of reflection and contemplation.

In a modest way, the volume of essays here presented seeks to participate in a discussion that has been gathering momentum in recent years. Whether it is a rediscovery and reaffirmation of traditional moral values that is wanted, or a search for radically new ways of understanding the problems of man and society, open and reasoned discussion must be the first step. The essays making up the volume are characterized by a unity of concern and a convergence of themes all being more or less central to the prevailing preoccupations of thinking people everywhere. The topical issues of inhumanity, of selfishness, of indifference, and of fanaticism and intolerance have found their way into these essays, and although some problems are marginal to some of the contributions, all receive, we hope, a fair hearing.

Beyond this unity of concern and convergence of themes, however, the volume represents no philosophical or ideological 'line' that the editors would wish to sell to an interested reading public. Our contributors (not excepting the editors here) hold different views on substantive questions of political morality as well as on the relative importance of the sundry concrete topics considered by each, not to mention their varying conceptions of the most appropriate methods with which to tackle given problems. We believe, however, that this catholicity of content aids the volume in fulfilling its primary purpose of providing a forum for stimulating debate and discussion. Further, in order to ensure that moral philosophy at least in this volume has a fair chance of reaching the 'market-place', we have endeavoured to present essays which are free of technical jargon and a narrow scholasticism. Though at times this may have resulted in a loss of profundity and a dilution of argument, there are ample compensations.

We launch the collection in the belief that its content will be found relevant to many of the pressing moral concerns of our society, and, as editors, we wish to record our sincere gratitude to our contributors for their willingness to participate in the project, and for their efforts in preparing their contributions.

Hull, July 1971   B.P.
   R.N.B.

CONTENTS

Introduction		7
W. H. Walsh	Open and Closed Morality	17
A. J. M. Milne	Reason, Morality and Politics	31
R. S. Downie	Realism and Self-interest as Political Themes	52
R. N. Berki	The Distinction between Moderation and Extremism	66
Bhikhu Parekh	Liberalism and Morality	81
Geoffrey Goodwin	An International Morality?	99
Geraint Parry	The Machiavellianism of the Machiavellians	114
H. B. Acton	Strikes, Trade Unions and the State	136
K. R. Minogue	Theatricality and Politics: Machiavelli's Concept of Fantasia	148
Index		163

CONTRIBUTORS

W. H. WALSH
Professor of Logic and Metaphysics, University of Edinburgh

A. J. M. MILNE
Reader in Philosophy, Queen's University, Belfast

R. S. DOWNIE
Professor of Moral Philosophy, University of Glasgow

R. N. BERKI
Lecturer in Political Studies, University of Hull

BHIKHU PAREKH
Lecturer in Political Studies, University of Hull

GEOFFREY GOODWIN
Montague Burton Professor of International Relations, London School of Economics and Political Science

GERAINT PARRY
Senior Lecturer in Government, University of Manchester

H. B. ACTON
Professor of Moral Philosophy, University of Edinburgh

K. R. MINOGUE
Reader in Political Science, London School of Economics and Political Science

Open and Closed Morality

W. H. WALSH

I begin by inviting attention to a common though generally unremarked feature of much current political controversy. When Americans differ about the defensibility of the American presence in Vietnam, or when (to take a far less significant but none the less typical example) British politicians debate the merits of a proposal to discontinue the provision of free milk to schoolchildren of a certain age, the parties to the argument tend to divide on the following lines.

On the one side is a group of self-proclaimed liberals[1] who see matters of this sort as black and white affairs, questions to which every honest man will at once know the answer. This is because we have here, as they see it, to do with problems which are primarily *moral*; we have to decide whether a set of actions or proposed actions is morally required, permissible or forbidden. For the liberal mind, questions of this kind are essentially easy to answer, since moral principles, which bind men as such, are patent for all to see. Moral decisions require no special insight, still less any special technical competence; they depend most of all on good will, and this is within the reach of us all.

Liberals will of course allow that to determine whether a course of action is right or wrong requires more than the adducing of moral

[1] The term 'liberal', like the term 'conservative', is used in this essay without special political overtones. Not all supporters of left-wing parties are liberals in the sense intended; indeed relatively few are out-and-out liberals. Thus in the Labour Party neither Mr Wilson nor Mr Callaghan is a fully committed liberal, though Mr Michael Foot and Mr Peter Shore perhaps are. Nevertheless, left-wing parties, particularly when out of office, have a standing tendency to appeal to liberal arguments. Similarly there are members of the Conservative Party who, as explained below, acknowledge the force of the liberal case, though the instinct of Conservatives is to embrace a different sort of philosophy. Those Conservatives who are seriously attracted by liberal ideas tend to leave the party, like Mr Humphrey Berkeley, or to leave politics, like Lord Boyle.

principles; it requires also a proper reading of the facts of the case. But in practice they mostly see the facts in cases of the kind under discussion as uncontroversial. Good men, the assumption is, have only to look at the evidence in an impartial way to discover how things really are and, once they have done that, the correct decision about desirability or the reverse follows almost with the compulsion of logic. To pretend that one could agree about the facts and advance another opinion about their value is quite indefensible; only someone who was fundamentally dishonest would attempt any such thing.

It follows from what I have said that liberals find it difficult, if not impossible, to treat their opponents on major political issues with even a minimum of respect. Obtuse and insensitive at best, the probabilities are that in most cases those who follow the anti-liberal line, are downright wicked. They are wicked because they must, if liberal assumptions are correct, know in their hearts that their cause is wrong, and yet refuse to acknowledge it. They suffer from the lie in the soul. Or less fancifully, they are engaged in pursuing their own interest or the interest of their class, in gratifying a lust for power or in other discreditable forms of conduct.

The frame of mind I have been describing is extremely common among American intellectuals today. The way they speak of members of the American government will illustrate what I mean when I say that liberals tend to regard their opponents with contempt. In their kinder moments they will perhaps describe President Nixon as a 'clown', as if he did not really know what he was doing; more commonly, however, they think of him as a morally guilty man. Nor is this attitude of moral contempt peculiar to America. Many liberals in this country have what is at bottom the same view of the Tory government and the Tory Party. They see them as men who, because of their readiness to supply arms to South Africa, to negotiate with Mr Ian Smith and (apparently) to dismantle the Welfare State, show that they are indifferent to the plainest moral principles. Moderate liberals might allow that exaggeration sometimes comes into these matters; the need to make continual political scenes forces political critics from time to time to profess a measure of indignation which they do not really feel. But even in cases of this kind it is rare for the feeling to be absent altogether. On the contrary, since the critics in question generally believe both that they themselves are indubitably right and that their opponents know that they are, indignation and contempt are never far from their minds.

What now of the other party in conflicts of this kind, which I shall for convenience call 'conservative'? The first thing that needs to be said is that they agree with their opponents in stressing the importance of moral considerations in questions of politics. Some of them, indeed, are prepared to go further and acknowledge the full range of liberal claims about morality: the view that the moral law binds men as men and not as members of any particular community, that what is ultimately right and ultimately wrong are matters of common knowledge, requiring no special skill for their discernment, and that it is hence only in their reading of the facts that decent men can be divided when it comes to deciding concrete issues.

There are some conservatives who believe, or apparently believe, that they can start from the same premises as their opponents and arrive at quite different conclusions about what to do. But the contempt with which this suggestion is dismissed by liberals makes it hard to suppose that it is the whole truth about the matter. Equally, the idea that there can be no such thing as sincere and honest opposition to liberal causes is one which the uncommitted outsider must view with scepticism. Moral decency in private matters is certainly not confined to liberals; why then should we suppose that only those who think along liberal lines can claim to be morally motivated when it comes to public affairs?

What I want to suggest is that conservatives are not immoral, but rather have their own kind of morality. For them morality is, first and foremost, an affair internal to a particular community rather than a phenomenon covering the whole of mankind. Their typical reaction to liberal criticism is to regard it as abstract. By this they mean that it does not take sufficient account of the actual facts of the situation in which it is put forward; it is, in a certain way, unreal. A cynic might suppose that this reaction amounts to an attempt to reject moral considerations altogether, to argue that political decisions should be based solely on expediency, but this, as already indicated, is a mistake. The conservative is as alive to the need to build a good society as his opponent. The difference comes out in that he, unlike the liberal, wants to make his own society as good as he can, rather than to construct some finally valuable Utopia. And it is central to the thought of the conservative that a society of any sort is an organic whole, in which no part can operate in entire independence of the rest. Hence the virtues on which conservatives insist are in the first instance communal virtues, and the vices they seek to avoid are modes of conduct which would disrupt social life as such.

Like their opponents, conservatives want to encourage conduct which is unselfish; unlike them they make play with the notion of the common good rather than that of the categorical imperative. They present aims as desirable not because they are demanded by universal moral law, but because they further purposes in which all right-thinking members of the community may be expected to be interested. And instead of speaking of rights which men possess in virtue of their sheer humanity, they feel the need to have regard to the welfare and wishes of their fellow-citizens, persons with whom they are joined in a continuing enterprise and who consequently have claims on them of an altogether closer kind than could rest on merely legal relationships.

It is only if we take account of facts of the sort here referred to that we can understand the arguments from which this essay started. One party to these arguments, the liberal group, as we have seen, has the conviction of being unshakeably correct. It rests its case on what seem to it to be cast-iron considerations of morality, and sees its opponents as, in various degrees, disingenuous and bad. That it takes this line provokes more bafflement than understanding in the other side, the conservatives, the more so because its members realize that, by their own standards at least, they are not totally indifferent to the public good and so, presumably, not entirely without virtue. What they need to observe is that conservatives and liberals are working within different traditions of morality. The morality of the conservative is a closed morality; it is the morality of a particular community. The morality of the liberal is an open morality; it is a morality which has nothing to do with any particular human groups, but applies to all men whatever their local affiliations.

Let us pursue this contrast further. Among the main tenets of liberal morality are these. First, that the moral law (itself a significant expression) holds without distinction of persons: it applies to *anyone* who finds himself in a certain situation. A moral question is one into which particularities cannot properly enter, for a man comes on the moral scene not as this individual but as someone who falls under a certain description. I cannot claim moral indulgence on the ground that *I* am a unique person (though I might on the ground that I am present in a capacity which is in fact unique), nor can I justify my behaviour to another on the ground that he has a special relationship to *me*. In other words, privilege and preferential treatment have no place in morality, which is a sphere of pure principle.

Secondly, that the moral law commands for its own sake and not for the sake of any good its observance produces or might be expected to produce, whether private or public. In liberal thought there is not only an absolute dichotomy between morality and expediency, but an equally sharp division between the right and the good. We are under absolute obligation to do what we see to be right, whether or not we think good will result from it. To start asking 'Why should I be moral?' is to show that you do not know what morality is; it is to open the door fatally to compromise and vice.

Thirdly, that a man's only overriding loyalty is to the moral law itself. To give special consideration to another person on the ground that one feels specially warm towards him (he is, for example, an old friend, or a fellow-countryman), or to treat someone with something less than fairness because he belongs to another group, is to fail to live up to the demands of morality. Hence there is no real place in this way of thinking for virtues like patriotism or loyalty as commonly understood: claims based on these grounds will lack all moral appeal. A liberal can admire the courage which leads a man to lay down his life for his country or his friend, but will be indifferent or even hostile if it turns out that what mattered in the sacrifice was the fact that it was *his* country or *his* friend. Love of country can be morally innocuous only if it is deprived of its exclusive features; that is to say, if it is seen as a condition which is not confined to members of a limited group, but would be thought admirable wherever it occurred.

The ideas just expressed are now so widely accepted among educated people in the Western world that it may come as a surprise to suggest that they are not definitive. Could someone repudiate or ignore the main principles of liberal morality and still claim to be moral? The answer to this is that there certainly have been, and are, societies and sub-societies in which the whole institution of morality has a very different look. The object of the institution in such societies is the same as in those where the liberal view prevails: to induce human beings to forgo immediate personal satisfactions and thus to act unselfishly. But whereas the liberal commends moral conduct as an end in itself, his conservative counterpart thinks of it as conducive to a good which is in some sense the agent's own good. As Plato put it, the point of acting morally is to get what one truly wants or (which he took to be the same thing) what is truly good for one; self-sacrifice is a form of self-realization.

The thinking behind this view is that men are constituted what they are by their social relations; it is only as parts of a wider whole that they can be understood or have the life they do. The individual dies, the community of which he is an intimate part continues, and in these circumstances the real wish of the individual must be that the community should prosper. For this to be possible, curbs must be placed on selfish and anti-social behaviour on the part of individual members of the community. Some of these have to be imposed with the force of the law; others become effective as a result of moral pressures. But though a society of this sort will operate a system of moral rules, it will neither take any of them to be absolute nor insist on their observance as a good in itself. In any concrete case the ultimate consideration will be not the character of the act done, but the question of how far it conduces to or impedes the realization of the common good. Moreover, it will be the practice in such societies to take account in specific moral decisions of a factor mentioned earlier in this paper, the close interdependence of members of the community as seen by those who take this view. The quasi-legal approach to morality favoured by liberals, according to which men appear on the moral scene as cases rather than individuals, will not be thought appropriate, since here we have to do not with persons who are otherwise indifferent to us, but with those who participate with us in a common life. To ignore this fact would be to ignore the whole basis of our social existence. It would be like asking the father of a family to treat his children as if they had nothing specially to do with him, when natural ties of love and common interest render such an attitude absurd. The relations between different members of a community are seen on the view I am presenting as at least analogous to those of a family. It is this, I think, that explains the insistence in societies of this sort on virtues like loyalty and solidarity which, as we have seen, make so little appeal to the liberal. To give special consideration in these circumstances to one's fellows is, so far from being immoral, something which is positively required. We expect our compatriots and other associates to behave towards us with loyalty and fellow-feeling, and in turn they have a right to the same sort of behaviour from us.

I have tried to give brief accounts of two ways of regarding morality or, if the description is preferred, of two conflicting moral systems. But it must be confessed that the wording just employed is controversial. Many liberal thinkers would simply deny that what I am calling closed or conservative morality is morality at all; for them it is just a form of higher selfishness. Now it is certainly true that the main assumptions of liberal thought on this subject are by now built into the moral outlook of educated Western men. It is hard in particular for a Western intellectual to divest himself of ideas like that of the moral law which applies without distinction of persons to men as men, or to question the belief that moral demands are ineluctable and must be accepted whatever the consequences to society or its members. But if we turn from the sphere of theory to that of fact we find a very different state of affairs. It might even be argued that morality normally takes the form of something internal to a particular society; open morality of the liberal kind, so far from being the norm, has a precarious and uncertain foothold at best.

Consider in this connection that remarkable phenomenon the Labour Movement. The very fact that it calls itself a 'movement' differentiates it from other political organizations and suggests that its members see themselves as concerned with something more significant than the pursuit of common interests. The Labour Movement is thought of by many of its supporters as engaged in a sort of crusade, a crusade whose object is to bring into existence an altogether better society than the one we have now. There can be no disputing the strongly moral nature of the main Labour objectives. Labour, as we are repeatedly told, is the party that cares, that condemns the existing social set-up as grossly unjust and aspires to produce conditions in which all citizens, whatever their walk of life, get treated decently and fairly. And no doubt it is this feature of the situation which attracts to the party the support of so many liberal-minded persons.

But though such persons are prominent in the counsels of the Movement, it cannot be said that their ideas dominate its activities. Many humble Labour supporters are happy to think that theirs is the cause of decency and justice, but are not willing to allow their day-to-day decisions to be determined solely by the precepts of universal morality. When it is a question of what to do in a particular case, another factor comes in: the fact that members of the Labour Movement form a special sub-society inside the wider British society, a sub-society which has its own particular loyalties and makes its own particular demands. As well as serving the cause of justice, the average Labour activist has also to serve the cause of the working man. In asking himself what should be done, he cannot ignore the fact that he and others are united in the pursuit of certain common ends. To some intellectuals this feature of the situation seems unimportant: when it comes to choosing between adhering to what they take to be morally right and being disloyal to their friends, they have no hesitation in preferring the former. Loyalty, as we have seen, never figured very high in the list of liberal virtues. But the sort of reaction decisions of this kind provoke in less intellectual members of the party is surely significant: they think of persons of this sort with distaste and distrust. The words 'scab' and 'blackleg' play a prominent part in the vocabulary of politically-committed working men. They carry with them overtones of extreme moral condemnation. And there can be little doubt that, for many staunch supporters of the Labour party, loyalty to the Movement as such takes precedence over all other considerations.

To condemn an opponent's move or policy as immoral in the liberal sense is one thing. To agree that if one's own practice is contrary to abstract justice it should be abandoned, at least where this means dissociating oneself from one's fellow-workers, is quite another. The very fact that workers repeatedly support striking colleagues in circumstances where negotiated agreements are flouted and where their own personal interests are in danger shows that the morality of this Movement is far more that of the second pattern sketched above than the first. It is a closed or restricted morality, a morality of a living but none the less limited community, rather than a morality of human nature as such.

If this is the state of affairs in Britain, a society in which liberal professions are continually voiced, can we expect it to be different in other parts of the world? Supporters of Black Power in the United States commonly appeal to considerations of universal morality in denouncing current American society, but it is increasingly clear that it is not their object to set up an abstractly just community. They want a good life for black men, not for human beings as such. Similarly Jews and Arabs in the Middle East each defend themselves by invoking universal moral principles, though it is plain that neither party regards itself as unconditionally bound by such principles. Each speaks in the name of humanity when it suits them, but has other allegiances as well. In cases where individual Jews or Arabs are accused of what the outside world calls 'atrocities', the chances are that their behaviour will be seen in a very different light by their compatriots. Nor can this circumstance be adequately explained by saying that the nation concerned is uniquely cynical and corrupt. The fact is, whether we like it or not, that we have to do here with actions which are wrong on one reckoning, but innocuous or even admirable on another. From the point of view of external observers (who incidentally live in quite different conditions) they will seem callous and inhumane; internal observers, by contrast, may think them everything they should be. Those who are within and of the group concerned see the preservation and prosperity of their community as the supreme good, and accordingly regard as praiseworthy any action which furthers that end and is done for the sake of that end. If such an action brings harm to the innocent, that will be regretted, but not to the extent that the action will be condemned.

Liberals who find this attitude shocking should reflect on a case which often engages their own sympathies, that of the Catholic community in Northern Ireland. Is it really clear that where divisions are as strong as they are in this instance a single universal moral law applies to both parties? Is it clear again that failure to acknowledge such a law (and that neither party acknowledges it in practice is an indisputed fact) means that the people concerned have no conception of morality? It seems to me obvious that the answer to both questions is 'no'. Catholics and Protestants in Northern Ireland have each an internal moral system of their own; both communities contain good and bad men. But to expect either to denounce its own members in the name of abstract moral principle is totally unrealistic, not just because it is to fail to take account of human nature, but more importantly because it is to misunderstand what morality is in practice. Denunciation of this kind, as we know from the experience of the United States today, has the effect of disrupting an entire community. A powerful group can, perhaps, survive the shock and benefit in the end; in the case of a weaker one it must necessarily be fatal.

That what I am calling 'closed morality' is a fact, seems to me beyond reasonable dispute. The curious thing, indeed, is that we commonly overlook this aspect of the moral scene. That we do so can be explained only by the confidence we feel in the moral preconceptions of advanced thinkers in our own society. Just as Christians in the halcyon days of the past believed that their religion, which had no ties with any particular nation or race, was the only true faith, so do many Western intellectuals believe that theirs is the only true morality. But, on one level at least, the belief is tenable in neither instance. As Vico argued, religion is a necessary, or at least an invariable, component of society in any form; a community without religion would perhaps not be human. But by the same token religion in its original form is part of the life of a particular community. The God of Israel who brought the Jews out of the house of bondage was notorious for acts of favour and disfavour towards his chosen people; it was only after the Christian era that he began to care for Gentiles. And though the Christian God is very different, not all his followers have forgotten the narrower basis from which the ecumenical outlook has developed. It is the same in the sphere of morals. There too we have the spectacle of a universal morality supervening on something which was originally much more localized, and which survives to an altogether greater extent than many moralists and philosophers are willing to allow. To leave this aspect of the situation out of the reckoning is to misunderstand the whole phenonemon of morality.

Yet it might be argued that, though this is important from one point of view, from another it has relatively little significance. I began this essay by referring to a series of political arguments which, I claimed, could be understood only if they were seen to involve a conflict between two different kinds of morality. But what follows if the point is granted? Suppose that it is agreed that the people I am calling 'liberals' and 'conservatives' in fact work with moral conceptions which diverge at important points: does this seriously weaken the liberal case or make the conservative attitude more palatable? No committed liberal would agree that it did. For he would maintain that, even if his opponent had a morality of a sort, it was demonstrably an inferior morality. Restricted morality may survive alongside universal morality, but no one with any degree of honesty could follow the precepts of the former when they conflict with those of the latter.

This argument raises some interesting questions. One is whether it is right in fact. Is it really true that no decent person could disregard the claims of universal morality if it meant, for example, proving disloyal to a friend? We have seen that, even in our society, there are areas in which comradeship and solidarity often matter more than fairness or principle. It is not clear that we can satisfactorily deal with this fact by dismissing the persons concerned as morally backward. But there is a second question which is more important, that of the criteria by which one is to decide that one moral system is superior to another.

One possible test might be that of *effectiveness*: a moral system might be said to have value in so far as it was widely accepted and acted on. By this test conservative morality is certainly entitled to some respect, for it is, in effect, morality in its original form, and it survives to a far greater extent than its critics allow. Not that liberal morality comes out badly by this test either. True, its hold on professed followers is often less than its devotees would wish: the pressures of a different kind of morality are constantly felt. Yet against this we can set the fact that those who belong to the other camp are sufficiently aware of their opponents' philosophy to be made uneasy when accused of disregarding principle. In general, we may say that open morality has more than a foothold in Great Britain, if not in Northern Ireland, and that if few accept it wholeheartedly, even fewer disregard it altogether. The same is presumably true of the rest of Western Europe and of large parts of North America, though less obviously of many other parts of the world.

A second test might be a test of *adaptability*. Bergson, who so far as I know was the first to talk about 'open' and 'closed' morality, associated the latter with routine and habit. He thought of a closed society as one which decides what to do exclusively by reference to what has been done in the past. Against that, open morality was the morality of innovators; it was a way of going on which could face change with confidence. But though it is true that many traditional societies with restricted moralities have been bound by habit in just this way, there seems to be no special reason why closed communities should not practise moral innovation. There are, after all, plenty of examples in history of limited groups which have shown a high degree of inventiveness on the technical plane; the modern Israelis are a conspicuous instance. Invention in one area can be matched by invention in another. A closed society need not be bound by its past, any more than it need refuse to admit all new blood from outside. The governing class in nineteenth-century Britain had a high sense of its own identity, but it was by no means hidebound, and it acted intelligently in opening its ranks to fresh talent. It might serve as a paradigm case of a restricted group which adapted itself to changing circumstances with conspicuous success.

Those who accept universal morality may indeed claim to be equipped with an apparatus for dealing with any moral problem that can crop up. Whatever action is proposed they have, as Kant said, 'only' to ask themselves if its maxim is capable of holding as a universal law. If it is not, the act can be ruled out as immoral. By contrast, it is said, those who accept a restricted morality must be limited in their moral possibilities: they will know how to cope with a set number of routine situations, but nothing else. They will consequently be completely nonplussed when confronted with the unfamiliar. For reasons already indicated, I do not fully subscribe to this criticism, though I admit that it has some force. But even if it were correct, that in itself would not establish the liberal case.

Whatever Kant may have thought, the test of the universalization of maxims is not easy to apply. As Miss Anscombe pointed out some years ago, you cannot discover the maxim of an action until you can agree on its description, and much of the difficulty in morals arises from the fact that the same actions are described by different parties in different terms. Robbing a man of what legally belongs to him is presumably not universalizable; taking from the rich to give to the poor may be. But there is a still more serious objection to the procedure, which is that it is not sufficiently decisive. On its own account it rules out certain courses of action as immoral, but does nothing to show which of a number of permissible actions should be undertaken. It would not help Sartre's youth to decide whether to stay with his mother in occupied France or to join the French forces abroad. And if that is admitted, the claim made by supporters of universal morality that they have a means of dealing with any moral problem is false.

Is not the fact that open morality is *universal* a decisive point in its favour? This question might be taken in different ways. It might in the first place have to do with the fact that morality of this sort is indefinitely extensible, that it can without difficulty embrace as many persons as care to accept it. Closed morality depends for its very existence on the existence of other social relations; until these are developed it cannot operate. For a closed society to forge moral relations with those outside its ranks is thus always a slow business. But we live in a world which, thanks to advances in technology, is far more of a unity than the world of the past. We need to have relations with persons and groups who, until the other day, were thought of by us as totally remote. Is not open morality manifestly superior at least in this respect?

The trouble with this argument is that it promises more than it can perform. Those who accept open morality are indeed prepared to regard themselves as part of a moral order which covers the whole of humanity. They will agree to treat anyone with whom they come into contact with moral respect. But will this attitude be reciprocated? It may and it may not. If someone were to announce in, say, Bristol that he proposed to conduct his life on the principle that man exists as an end in himself, he would certainly find others to go along with him. If he were to make the same announcement in Belfast or in Famagusta the response might well be different. It could be that the only effective way of developing moral relations between communities which are deeply divided is to let them rub along together as best they can. Moral relationships spring out of relationships of convenience. The fact that I need to co-operate for economic purposes with someone from another group may in the end induce me to consider widening my society to include him, or at least to regard him as something better than a total outsider. In the meantime, talk about the rights of man will not necessarily affect me at all.

But there is another way of taking this third suggested test: as having to do with the *content* of morality. As has already been mentioned, few partisans of open morality would be prepared to take its rival with any degree of seriousness; on the contrary, they would regard it with contempt. Their ground for doing this would lie in its disregard of what they see as the most basic moral principle of all, the principle that in the moral sphere all human beings are equally worth while. Open morality, in their opinion, is clearly superior in that it recognizes, as does no other system, what is sometimes called the infinite worth of the human person. Leave this out, and what you are left with is not a morality at all.

Now it is open to conservatives at this point to reply that the argument begs the question. It assumes that what the liberal takes to be obvious will be universally agreed to be such. All the indications are that this is simply not true. Nor is it only in the benighted ranks of Northern Irish Protestants that the principle that humanity is entitled to respect is ignored. The followers of Chairman Mao are also lukewarm about it, as is shown in their treatment of 'enemies of the people'. But instead of pressing this point I should like to turn to another, that of the justification for this basic liberal conviction.

What kind of answer can the liberal give to someone who asks why we should accept the principle that men are entitled to moral respect simply in virtue of their humanity? Three answers can be suggested. First, that the principle is self-evident and needs no justification. This answer fails because the principle is not universally taken to be self-evident. The more people think it is, the stronger will the argument become. It remains true, even so, that at present we are a long way from unanimity on the point.

Secondly, it might be argued that the belief that man is an end in himself connects with and can be justified in terms of the Christian beliefs that we are all God's creatures and that Jesus Christ died for all men, Jew and Gentile, bond and free. That there is a connection between the two, in the sense of a historical link, seems indisputable. Universal morality developed in conditions where Christian views were still widely held; it would not be entirely fanciful to see it as in essence a secular deposit or survival of Christianity. But of course it is one thing to trace a historical link and another to find an internal connection. Few, if any, supporters of universal morality would want to argue that you could not be moral unless you were Christian. It is a central tenet of this system of thought that morality is 'autonomous', which means amongst other things that 'this is right' cannot be reduced to 'this is commanded by God'. For most liberals the existence of God is irrelevant to the question of what obligations we have. To justify any particular moral conviction by reference to it is hence hardly plausible.

Finally, there is the line taken by Kant, who connected the unconditional worth of man with his possession of a sense of morality, and sought to make the latter intelligible in terms of a contrast between two different worlds. Human beings, in Kant's view, have a dual nature; to put the point in popular terms, they are at once flesh and spirit. As sensuous beings possessed of bodies they belong to the material or natural order, the world Kant himself called 'phenomenal'. But they also have minds and above all wills, and thanks to that can conceive of themselves as belonging to another order altogether, a spiritual order which has its own laws just as the natural order has. The feeling of moral compunction, according to Kant, is an effect in the phenomenal world of the fact that man is not just a natural but also a rational being. It points to something beyond the material order, whose existence has to be assumed for purposes of action, even though it cannot be known or even treated as a real possibility from the theoretical point of view.

Kant's position on these matters is a subtle one, to which no short summary can do justice. But we do not need to examine it in detail in order to be able to pose the vital question about it for our present purposes. According to Kant, morality has to do, not with human wants or needs, but with the fact that every human being is also a rational being. Each of us belongs, in one aspect of himself, to a world of pure spirits. As such he is subject to non-natural influences, and this comes out in his moral behaviour. The question to ask is whether we must, or even can, accept this strange metaphysical dualism as a basis for making sense of the moral life. For my part I find that I must answer this question in the negative. As I see it, morality has to do with the here and now. It is in the everyday world of space and time that moral decisions are made and moral struggles take place. To explain an important part of what goes on here by reference to another world altogether seems entirely otiose. Nor do I see how modern liberals, most of whom are naturalistic in their metaphysical outlook, could draw much support from Kant's system of ideas. But if Kant is unable to support them, who or what can?

My purpose in raising these questions has not been to discredit open morality. Like other educated persons in this country I am deeply influenced by it and am moved by its demands even in cases where I doubt its total authority. Rather, what I have wanted to suggest is that the moral situation, even in Britain but much more obviously in some other parts of the world, is far more complicated than the liberal supposes. Liberal morality has supervened on an older morality which is still practised and is still entitled to respect. We can neither deal with fundamental moral conflicts in a practical way nor theorize about morals successfully unless we take that fact into account.

Reason, Morality and Politics

A. J. M. MILNE

This is an essay in political philosophy in the sense that its central theme is the concept of politics. Conceptual questions are the traditional subject-matter of philosophy and typically take some such form as: 'What can be meant by . . .?' and: 'How should we think of . . .?' I am asking them about politics, especially the second sort: 'How should we think of politics?' and in particular, 'From what perspective should we regard it?' Hence the other words in my title: 'Reason' and 'Morality'. The perspective must be justified on rational grounds, which means, as we shall see later, that in an important sense it has to be a moral one. But is there any problem about the concept of politics? The word is in current use. Most people know well enough for practical purposes what it covers. They can recognize political issues, to say nothing of politicians, when they encounter them. But this is not the point. The fact that a word is in current use shows only that people have uses for it, not that they fully and clearly understand all that it expresses. There may well be latent ambiguities and inconsistencies of which they are unaware.

However matters may be on the practical plane, two books by influential writers point to a theoretical problem. These are Bertrand De Jouvenel's *The Pure Theory of Politics*[1] and Bernard Crick's *In Defence of Politics*.[2] Not only are their concepts of politics different, but both are unsatisfactory for reasons which I shall explain more fully but which roughly come to this. De Jouvenel's pure theory is as much a theory of advertising as of politics. Crick's defence seems more appropriate to industrial relations in a free enterprise economy than to politics. Both have failed to bring out the vital point, 'What makes politics "political"?', which suggests that the concept of politics is more elusive and harder to characterize than might be supposed. This in turn suggests that one

[1] New Haven, Yale University Press, 1963.
[2] Weidenfeld and Nicholson, 1962.

reason for trouble in practical politics may lie in conceptual confusion. Misconceiving its character, people expect too much, too little, or else the wrong things, from politics.

Whether the conceptual investigations of political philosophy can influence these expectations is another matter. Perhaps it is not too much to hope that their influence, if any, will be beneficial. At all events, I shall present my own account of the concept of politics in the later stages of this essay, paving the way first with some comments on De Jouvenel and Crick, especially the latter, and then with a discussion of law and morality. But a cautionary word about my treatment of these writers is necessary. It is incomplete and one-sided, since it concentrates on my disagreement with them. I have not the space to dwell on what I agree with and admire in their work, which in each case is considerable.

1. De Jouvenel's concept of politics is wide in scope. 'I hold the view that we should regard as political every systematic effort performed at any place in the social field to move other men in pursuit of some design cherished by the mover.'[1] Two stages are always involved: instigation and response. After analysing instigation, he comments: 'It is important to stress that no mention has been made of the state, of sovereignty, of the constitution, or functions of public authority, of political obligation etc. . . .'[2] The omission is deliberate. De Jouvenel thinks that most people's ideas of politics are too narrow. 'In fact what is commonly thought of as politics is merely a natural necessary outgrowth of fundamentally political relations which spontaneously arise whenever men are brought together and thereby given the opportunity to act upon one another. There is no difference in nature between social relations and political relations. It is just a matter of relations between men.'[3]

The key idea in Crick's concept of politics is conciliation, an essential part of which is readiness to compromise. But politics is not just any kind of conciliation. First there must be government, which is 'the organization of a group of men in a given community for survival.'[4] Politics is essentially connected with government. But the existence of government does not guarantee that there will be politics. On the contrary: 'It is unknown in any but advanced and complex societies and it has specific origins found only in European experience.'[5] What then is it? According to Crick: 'Politics can simply be defined as the activity by which differing interests in a given unit of rule are conciliated by giving

[1] De Jouvenel, op cit., p. 30.
[2] ibid., p. 81.
[3] ibid., p. 82.
[4] Crick. op. cit., p. 22.
[5] ibid., p. 13.

them a share in power in proportion to their importance to the welfare and survival of the whole community.'[1] Why should there be politics? His answer is that 'Politics arises from the fact of the simultaneous existence of different groups, hence different interests and traditions, in a territorial unit under a common rule.'[2] It follows that a distinction must be drawn between politics and diplomacy. Crick concedes that 'The will to conciliate and compromise may actually be stronger in international relations.'[3] But the lack of any international government to ensure stability and order means that diplomacy can only be quasi-politics.

The word 'theory' in De Jouvenel's title is intended to 'perform the representative function which the word "theory" evokes in the factual sciences.'[4] This representative function 'constitutes in the mind a sort of model of what occurs in observable reality, a necessary attempt to reduce phenomenal diversity to intellectual simplicity.'[5] He says that 'The adjective "pure" in the title is used by analogy with the contrast between "pure" and "organic" in chemistry. Just as organic bodies are far more complex than those to which the student is first introduced in a beginner's course in pure chemistry, so are the situations and relations of actual politics far more complex than those examined here.'[6] Attempting to forestall criticism, he continues: 'Therefore the reader should not complain that the whole of reality is not encompassed. Because my purpose is to come down to the greatest possible degree of simplicity, political phenomena appear essentially as relations between individuals.'[7] Hence his concept of politics: it has been framed to suit his purpose. But that does not make it acceptable.

The trouble with his model is that it is not strictly one of politics at all. The salesman, the religious evangelist, and the blackmailer, are all of them systematically trying to move other men, but in pursuit of very different designs. We need a criterion which differentiates between 'political' and other designs. De Jouvenel's concept of politics fails to provide one, which is not to deny that instigation and response are important in politics as in other fields. But that is another matter.

Crick's concept of politics is not open to the same objection. He delimits the political sphere, differentiating between it and others which resemble it such as diplomacy. There are, however, other grounds for criticism. These have to do with his concept of government and also

[1] ibid., p. 16.
[2] ibid., p. 14.
[3] ibid., p. 23.
[4] De Jouvenel, op cit., p. 31.
[5] ibid., p. 30.
[6] ibid., p. x (preface).
[7] ibid., p. x (preface).

with his emphasis on conciliation. But there is also something else which I will deal with first because it is important for my own argument. Crick denies that for there to be politics 'there must be already in existence some shared ideal or common good: some consensus or "consensus juris".'[1] If there is any such thing as the common good, it lies in the practice of politics itself. 'It is not some external and intangible spiritual adhesive or some allegedly objective general will. These are misleading notions of how a community holds together.'[2] The true explanation is simpler and more mundane. 'But different groups hold together firstly because they have a common interest in survival, secondly because they practise politics, not because they agree about fundamentals, or some such concept too vague, too personal, or too divine, to do the job of politics for it.'[3]

But the idea of 'agreement about fundamentals' cannot be dismissed so easily. Admittedly the phrase is elliptical. It implies more than it says. But what is implied is true and important, as the case of South Africa shows. European South Africans are unwilling to conciliate, much less to compromise with, other ethnic groups in the country. They fear that if they do, they will lose their separate identity and cease to exist as a distinctively European group. Their interest in survival does not create common ground between them and Africans, 'Coloureds', or Asians. There is no 'agreement about fundamentals' between these different ethnic groups in the sense that they cannot agree upon a way of life in which all of their respective members can share as fellow-citizens in a wider South African community. Consequently there is no such community, and South Africa remains a deeply and painfully divided country.

The trouble in Crick's account lies in his phrase 'common interest in survival'. Whose survival and in what form? If a number of different groups each wants to survive, they can be described as having a common interest in survival in the sense that an interest in survival is a characteristic possessed by each of them and therefore common to them all. But the possession of this common characteristic does not mean that they can hold together as a community. They may want to survive in mutually incompatible ways, so that the survival of one is possible only at the expense of the survival of others. There is another sense, however, in which a common interest in survival is relevant to the existence of a community. It is simply that if different groups are to hold together as a community, they must have a common interest in the survival of that community, not merely in their own survival as separate groups.

[1] Crick, op. cit., p. 19.
[2] ibid., p. 19.
[3] ibid., p. 19.

This means that if a community is to hold together, its members must want to live together despite their differences, and must be able and willing to maintain institutions and practices through which they can do so. Their primary loyalty must be to the community, not to particular groups or classes within it. Obligations to it must take precedence over obligations to them if a conflict arises. More generally the ideas, beliefs and values which the members share must be more important to them than those which divide them; a state of affairs which can be briefly if elliptically expressed by saying that there is agreement about fundamentals among them.

This however has the drawback of suggesting a static picture. It emphasizes the 'state of affairs' which must exist in a community to enable it to hold together. But modern industrial communities are not static. They undergo social and cultural changes which are often far-reaching in character. Social and cultural changes are usually interdependent, changes in institutions, practices and social relations going hand in hand with changes in ideas, beliefs and values. This prompts the question: how can a community hold together during such changes when the state of affairs which enables it to hold together is itself part of what changes? The short answer is that changes in this state of affairs must occur gradually over a period of time. They must be piecemeal not wholesale, so as to provide some continuity among the ideas, beliefs and values which the members of the community share. This is in fact what invariably happens. It is hard to conceive of wholesale cultural change at a moment of time. It would involve replacing at a stroke a community's language, together with all its familiar habits of thought and action.

All this admittedly only scratches the surface of the problem of social change. But it is enough to show that what is implied in 'agreement about fundamentals' is compatible with the fact of social change. The matter may be put by saying that while there must be agreement about fundamentals at a given time, this does not preclude gradual change over time in the fundamentals about which there is agreement. I referred just now to loyalty and to obligations. These are moral concepts, and it is time to turn to the subject of morality and along with it that of law, itself an important factor in maintaining continuity through change.

2. There is an obvious difference between law and morality. If I am discovered acting illegally, I shall be brought before a court and, depending upon my offence, either punished or made to pay compensation. But if I am discovered acting immorally although not illegally, for instance lying or breaking a promise, there is no court to sentence me. I shall

THE MORALITY OF POLITICS

probably incur disapproval and perhaps hostility, but that is all. Law is backed by official sanctions imposed and carried out by judicial and penal authorities. Morality is backed only by the informal sanction of public opinion. But this is far from being the whole story. It tells us nothing about the positive relation between law and morality, and nothing about the duty to obey the law. Something must be said about all this if the justification for the sanctions behind the law is to be understood.

Morality is prior to law in the sense that there can be morality without law, but not law without morality. While law can create particular obligations, it cannot create the general obligation or duty to obey law. A law prescribing obedience to law would be pointless. It presupposes the very thing it is intended to create: the general obligation to obey law. That obligation is necessarily moral, not legal, in character. Law can come into being only where morality is already a going concern; that is, in a community most of whose members acknowledge that they have moral obligations and are able and willing to carry them out. Obligation is the key notion in morality. To say of someone that he is under a moral obligation to do something, is to say that he ought to do it whether he wants to or not. Morality must be distinguished from self-interest, although the two can often coincide. It may be in my self-interest to do what I have a moral obligation to do. But the fact that it is in my self-interest cannot be the reason why I morally ought to do it. What then can be the reason? What is the rational ground for morality and its obligations?

Morality has a rational basis in certain conditions necessary for human co-operation: that is, co-operation between self-conscious beings capable of communication, decision and choice. People who co-operate together become dependent upon one another. Each must do his part if their common enterprise is not to break down. There can be co-operation therefore only where there is trust, and trust presupposes honesty. Being honest means acknowledging and meeting certain obligations: keeping your word, not lying, deceiving or stealing. Without the commitment to honesty and to the obligations it entails, there can be no trust, and hence no co-operation. Other commitments are also necessary: for instance, self-control and refraining from violence. A man who cannot control himself cannot be trusted. Violence wrecks co-operation.

But is there an inescapable commitment to co-operation? Yes, if there is an inescapable commitment to social living, because co-operation is of the essence of social life. I can rationally reject the commitment to co-operation and to the obligations it entails only if I am prepared to withdraw completely from all forms of association with other people, which presumably means either committing suicide or becoming a hermit, if the latter is still a live option in the world today.

Two empirical considerations are relevant. The first is that, as a matter of fact, morality is found in every human community. Everywhere there are recognized rules and standards to which people are expected to conform, and recognized virtues which they are expected to cultivate. The second concerns what has been called 'the diversity of morals'.[1] Everywhere there is morality but not the same morality. In different places and at different times, people have recognized different rules, standards and virtues. This diversity in the content of moral codes is found not only between different communities but between different groups and classes within the same community. Can it be reconciled with what was said in the last paragraph about co-operation and its moral commitments? Yes, because human co-operation can take many different forms and generate many different ways of life.

Historically, two factors have been especially important: differences in religious belief and in methods of production and economic relations. One need not be a Marxist to admit the latter point. But granted that these and other cultural differences have led to differences in the content of moral codes, the diversity cannot be absolute. Certain moral commitments with their attendant obligations are necessary for any kind of human co-operation whatever. These must first be acknowledged before there can be other values which vary. This is an *a priori* not an empirical thesis. It cannot be refuted by pointing to a community in which honesty and self-control are not recognized moral obligations. That would be to point to a community in which co-operation was breaking down, and which was losing its identity as a human community properly so called.

But diversity in the content of moral codes is found not only between different communities, but also between different groups and classes in the same community. Can a community hold together in the face of internal moral diversity? Isn't this likely to have a socially disintegrating effect? Not necessarily. It may be due to religious differences which are accepted as part of a way of life in which religious freedom and mutual toleration are basic principles. It may reflect the different standards of sexual conduct prevailing in different classes. This need not have a disintegrating effect if sexual relations are largely confined within each social class. But if internal moral diversity is not to have a disintegrating effect, it must be contained within a wider moral framework which is generally accepted; which brings us back to 'agreement about fundamentals'. Primary loyalty must be to the community, not to particular groups or classes within it. The ideas, beliefs and values which the

[1] M. Ginsberg, *'On the Diversity of Morals'*. London, Heinemann, 1956.

members share must be more important to them than those which divide them.

It may be objected that all this implies moral relativism. Provided there is basic agreement, it does not matter what the agreement is about. One way of life is morally as good as another. Where there is failure to agree, as in South Africa, there is no question of blame. It is not the fault of any one group but simply a fact. But granted that what has been said so far implies moral relativism, it is not the whole story. Rational appraisals of a community's way of life and of its particular moral code can be made on other grounds, for instance, enlightenment in the sense of coherence, knowledge and understanding. How far do a community's institutions and practices rest upon relevant scientific knowledge? How far are they free from internal inconsistencies? How far do they reflect insight and compassion?

I have not the space here to enlarge on this.[1] It is enough to point out that the view of morality presented here does not preclude rational criticism. Nor does it preclude assessing responsibility for the failure to reach agreement where this can be traced to obscurantism, prejudice, or superstition, or simply group selfishness.

To return to law. A community which has a system of law is morally committed to the general principle of the rule of law. This can be summarized in three specific principles: the supremacy of law, equality before the law, and freedom under the law. The supremacy of law means that the obligation to obey the law takes precedence over all other obligations. Legal rules override all other rules. All activities, all forms of voluntary association, together with their moral commitments, must be kept within the framework of what is permitted by the law. The other two principles are corollaries of the first. Equality before the law means the equal subjection of all to the authority of the law, including the government. When the law is changed, it must be done in the legally prescribed manner, and the same is true of the enforcement of the law. But if no one is above the law, by the same token no one is below it. All are equally entitled to the protection of the law and to whatever facilities it affords. Freedom under the law means that nothing is compulsory which is not legally prescribed or prohibited. Where the law is silent, everyone is free to act according to his own decision and choice. Legal sanctions are to be used only against law-breakers.

But why should there be law at all? What is the point of having a legal system? There are two fundamental reasons. The first is security. Personal safety and the safety of property is achieved better by law than by leaving it to the private efforts of individuals. There is of course a

[1] I have discussed this more fully elsewhere. See my *Freedom and Rights*. London, Allen and Unwin, 1968. Especially Chapters 3 and 7.

moral obligation to respect the security of persons and property. It is entailed by the obligations to be honest and to refrain from violence. But people do not always act morally, and security is too important a matter to leave to the personal morality of individuals. The presumption is that in fact most people will respect security without being required to do so by law. But for those who are unable or unwilling to meet this moral obligation, the law is there with its sanctions.

The second reason is that a system of law enables a community to organize and regulate its affairs for the benefit of all its members. Law is a method of social co-operation for attaining public ends which either could not be attained at all without it, or attained only partially and imperfectly.

Does not all this make law dependent on agreement about fundamentals, since there can be law only where there is a community and a community presupposes such agreement? What about South Africa? I said earlier that there is no South African community. But there is a South African legal system. It was that system which originally enacted and now enforces *apartheid*. The short answer is that it is the Europeans in South Africa who have a legal system, not the other ethnic groups in the country. There is enough agreement about fundamentals among European South Africans to enable them to hold together as a community and maintain a system of law. Their military and technological superiority has enabled them to impose this system upon the rest of the country and, through it, their ideas about how the other ethnic groups should live.

But while Europeans acknowledge the moral commitment to the rule of law, Africans, 'Coloureds' and Asians do not. What to Europeans is a legal system, to these groups is a system of discrimination and oppression. For the most part they obey it as the lesser evil, but do not acknowledge any moral obligation to support it. The conclusion to be drawn is this. Where there is no agreement about fundamentals, there can be no genuine community. But there can be an ersatz or pseudo-community held together by the superior force of one group which imposes its will upon the rest. South Africa is probably the most notorious case. But it is only one of a number of ersatz communities in the modern world.

What has been said about law and morality in this section is of course far from being the whole story. But it is sufficient for what I want to say later and to reinforce my criticism of Crick's account of what holds a community together. It was not for this reason however that I suggested that his concept of politics was open to criticism. Rather, it was his concept of government and his emphasis upon conciliation. According to him, governing a community means providing for its survival. This is too narrow. It ignores characteristic features of modern government. Let us try instead thinking of government as the activity of identifying and promoting the public interest at home and the national interest abroad. The key idea here is that of the public interest.[1] My thesis, which I shall try to defend in the rest of this essay, is that when properly understood, this idea is the rational basis of both government and politics.

3. A nation is not an individual 'writ large'. But in certain respects, the national interest abroad is comparable to the self-interest of an individual. Individual self-interest has a rational basis in the conditions necessary for personal well-being. In the modern Western world such conditions include an adequate income, some form of congenial work or occupation, access to facilities for recreation or leisure pursuits. It is in a man's self-interest to try to secure them. The national interest abroad has a rational basis in those conditions abroad which are necessary for the protection and prosperity of the nation. These include access to foreign markets, the maintenance of diplomatic relations with foreign governments, and the strategic disposition of military forces. It is in a nation's interest for steps to be taken to secure these conditions. When the same conditions are in the self-interest of a number of people, they have an interest in common. People can have a common interest without being aware of the fact. But when they are aware of it, this is a rational basis for co-operation. When conditions which are in the self-interest of some people are contrary to the self-interest of others, there is a conflict of interest between them. There are only two ways in which such conflicts can be resolved. Either one party must give way, or they must compromise. The incentive to compromise may be either prudential or moral: prudential when both parties are strong, so that neither can easily make the other give way, moral when each acknowledges the justice of the other's case.

All this is true of nations as well as of individuals. There are both common interests and conflicts of interest among them. But partly because a nation is not an individual 'writ large', the concept of self-interest is not helpful in understanding the idea of the public interest at home. For that, we must turn to what I shall call the 'corporate interest' of a voluntary association.

There are many kinds of voluntary association: clubs, churches, universities, political parties and trades unions, are familiar instances. But however much they differ, in every case there is some activity or range of activities, which is the association's *raison d'être*. Common self-interest is an obvious incentive to voluntary association, but it is by no means the only one. Mutual enjoyment, shared tastes, cultural, religious

[1] cf. Milne, op. cit., Chapter 8.

and moral convictions, are others. There can be as many kinds of voluntary association as there are kinds of activity in which people can share and associate to carry on together. The corporate interest of a voluntary association is an interest which all its members have in their capacity as members. It has a rational basis in the conditions which must be established and maintained within the association to enable the activity which is its *raison d'être* to be carried on successfully, that is, in a way which will enable all its members to participate in and contribute to it so far as they can. It is in the corporate interest of the association and therefore in the interest of each of its members qua members, that all of them should co-operate in establishing and maintaining these conditions.

This points to a moral dimension. Each member is responsible to all the rest for playing his part in upholding the corporate interest. In a club, each member has an obligation to obey the rules in the spirit as well as the letter, and to take his turn helping in necessary administrative chores, serving on committees and the like. The corporate interest of a voluntary association cannot conflict with the interest of its members qua members. They are necessarily the same. But this is not to say that the corporate interest and the self-interest of each member qua individual, are always the same. Much as a man may enjoy membership of a club, it may be too expensive or time-consuming. It is not in his self-interest to remain a member. Interest qua member and interest qua individual can conflict.

A nation is a territorial community into which successive generations of human beings are born, grow up and in the great majority of cases, live out their lives. This is of course not the whole story about nationhood. It says nothing about what differentiates modern nations from other kinds of human community, for instance, tribes, kingdoms, city states, empires, and the principalities and duchies of medieval Europe. But it is sufficient for my present purpose. We have seen that if a community is to hold together, its members must want to live together despite their differences, and must be able and willing to maintain institutions and practices through which they can do so. Primary loyalty must be to the community, not to particular groups, classes, or for that matter, voluntary associations, within it.

All this points to a sense in which a nation has a corporate interest comparable in certain respects with the corporate interest of a voluntary association. Its rational basis is in the conditions within the nation which are necessary to enable its common life to be maintained and developed, and especially in those necessary to enable all the members of the national community to participate in its common life in ways consistent with their status as members. What these ways are depends partly upon the material and economic circumstances prevailing within the nation, but also upon the ideas, beliefs and values which the members share and especially upon those which define the terms of their status as members. It is in the interest of the members of the national community in their corporate capacity as members, although not necessarily in the individual self-interest of each – about which more in a moment – that these conditions should be established and maintained. Each therefore has a responsibility arising out of his primary loyalty to the national community, to co-operate in establishing and maintaining them.

The phrase 'the public interest at home' is suitable to designate the corporate interest of a nation: 'at home' to contrast it with the national interest abroad; 'public' to contrast it with the self-interest of each member as an individual, with the corporate interests of voluntary associations within the national community, as well as with the common interests of sections and classes. These latter are 'private' in the sense that they are the proper concern only of individuals, of voluntary associations, and of particular sections and classes. The corporate interest of the national community is 'public' in the sense that it is the proper concern of all the members qua members.

Two qualifications however are necessary. The first is that, although distinct, the public interest at home and the national interest abroad are interdependent in the sense that they interact with and react upon each other. Economic prosperity in which all can share is in the public interest at home. Where foreign trade is important to the national economy, this means that it is in the national interest abroad to secure and keep foreign markets; which in turn means that it is in the public interest at home to prevent inflation and secure, so far as possible, price and wage stability.

The second concerns the relation between private interests and the public interest. The former can properly remain private in the sense of being the concern alone of those whose interests they are, only so long as they are not contrary to the public interest. If conflicts of sectional or class interests lead to violence, or threaten the health or safety of other people not belonging to the sections or classes involved, the resolution of such conflicts ceases to be a purely private matter. It is in the public interest that they should be resolved in ways which do no harm.

It may be objected that such conflicts betray unenlightened ideas of private interests. It can never really be in the self-interest of an individual, a section, or a class, to endanger the national community. Perhaps not. But the objection is mistaken if it is taken to mean that when both are properly understood, the public interest and private interests are essentially complementary and that no genuine conflicts between them can arise.[1] Matters are not so simple. A man's private interests are the interests he has, not as a member of his national community, but as an individual person and as a member of voluntary associations. He is also a member of the national community and pursues his private interests within the framework of its common life. But so far as his private interests are concerned, it does not matter to him whether all his fellow-citizens are participating in the national life in ways consistent with their status as members. All that matters is that the conditions prevailing in the national community should be such as to enable him to pursue his private interests successfully. He can afford to be indifferent to the lot of the perhaps millions of his fellow-citizens who are not directly involved in his private interests, so long as they do not bother him by interfering with his pursuit of his individual self-interest and with the activities of voluntary associations to which he belongs.

What is overlooked in the idea that private interests and the public interest are essentially complementary is simply this. When a man thinks about the life of his nation solely from the standpoint of his private interest, what concerns him is that there should be conditions in which his own particular private interests should prosper, not conditions which enable all his fellow-citizens to share in the national life on proper terms. While there is certainly much common ground between these two sets of conditions, they can never be wholly identical. This is because in no community is there a pre-established social harmony which guarantees that, always and everywhere, the maximum personal well-being of each is compatible with the maximum personal well-being of all.

It would be a mistake to describe the perspective of private interests as non-moral, much less as immoral. It has a moral dimension arising out of the responsibilities of membership in voluntary associations and from the obligations entailed in co-operating with other people in pursuit of common interests. But it is morally defective in comparison with the perspective of the public interest. The latter is the perspective of a man who thinks about the life of his nation not merely as an individual person but as a member of the national community, that is, the community to which his primary loyalty is due.[2] It is this primary loyalty which is the rational and the moral justification for giving precedence to the demands of the public interest when they conflict with

[1] Brian Barry in his essay 'The Public Interest' in A. Quinton (ed.), *Political Philosophy*, Oxford Readings in Philosophy, 1970, fails to bring out the point which follows below. For him, if I understand him rightly, the public interest is simply the common interest in my sense of the members of the national community, that is, their common self-interest qua individuals not qua members.

[2] For reasons of brevity I am ignoring loyalties wider than the nation. They would involve modifying my argument but not, I think, fundamentally changing it.

private interests. The public interest must have priority. Private interests must be adjusted to meet its requirements, not vice versa.

Another objection, apparently more far-reaching, is the whole comparison between a voluntary association and a nation. Agreement is to be expected in a voluntary association because people join it from choice. If they disagree, they can leave. But immigrants apart, people do not join a nation. They are born into it and by the time they have become capable of choice, are already caught up in its life. Agreement of the sort found in a voluntary association is therefore not to be expected. Have I not myself drawn attention to the case of the ersatz community where such agreement is manifestly lacking? Now I acknowledge that in an ersatz community, there can be no public interest properly so called. Instead, the common interest of the dominant group, for instance European South Africans, is likely to be imposed upon subordinate groups and represented by them as the public interest. It may also be true that few, if any, modern nations are without some ersatz characteristics, that is, without some alienated people in their midst whose primary loyalty is not to the national community. That, however, only means that no modern nation is more than an approximation to a genuine community. It does not invalidate the idea of the public interest. The more a nation approximates to being a genuine community, the more relevant this idea. Not only that. The more successfully the public interest is promoted, the better are the nation's prospects of becoming more of a genuine community.

But to return to the comparison between a voluntary association and a nation. Identifying in detail the conditions which are in the corporate interest of the former is unlikely to be much of a problem, even if establishing them sometimes may be. With the public interest in a modern industrial nation, the situation is different. The larger the scale and the greater the complexity of the national life, the more problems there are likely to be in identifying in detail just what conditions are necessary to enable all the members to participate in that life on proper terms. Problems are also likely in deciding how best to secure them once they have been identified. Corresponding problems of both sorts are also likely with respect to the national interest abroad. Now in a voluntary association, responsibility for identifying and promoting the corporate interest is usually vested in a management committee or similar agency. The members have a responsibility to co-operate but they must know what in particular is required of them. Hence the need for central guidance and direction if they are to co-operate intelligently and effectively. But if this is necessary in the case of a voluntary association where the problems are relatively simple, how much more is it necessary in the case of a nation? That was why I suggested at the end of the last section that the activity of governing should be thought of in terms of identifying and promoting the public interest at home and the national interest abroad.

According to Crick, governing a community means providing for its survival. This clearly falls within the scope of government in terms of the view I am recommending. Indeed it is one of those matters which is not in principle problematic. Internal peace and order, the security of person and property, are always in the public interest because in their absence any form of social life becomes precarious. As far as external threats are concerned, it is always in the national interest abroad to make diplomatic and if necessary, military arrangements to minimize them. But to think of government solely in terms of survival is to render unintelligible much of the scope of government action in contemporary Western nations. This typically includes the provision of services in fields such as education, housing, health, social welfare, communications and transport; the overall guidance and supervision of the economy; and, perhaps belatedly, measures for the preservation of the environment. Possibly the last can be construed in terms of providing for survival but hardly the rest.

If viewed in the perspective of the public interest however, this scope of government action becomes intelligible. I am not suggesting that it was because Western governments began thinking of themselves in terms of the idea of the public interest, that the scope of their action has come to be what it now is. Possibly a version of this idea may have played some part, albeit implicitly. But my point is not a historical one. Rather, it is that the idea of the public interest is the relevant criterion for critically appraising both the general scope of government action and particular government measures.

I am therefore proposing a normative theory of government. To say that the idea of the public interest is the relevant criterion for appraising government action is to say that it would be better if government was carried on in terms of that idea. But although normative it is not arbitrary. There are good reasons for it and I have tried to indicate them. It is also an interventionist theory. I am committed to saying that government ought to intervene in the national life to try to secure those conditions which it judges to be in the public interest. But while interventionist, it is at the same time a theory of limited government. The onus is on government to justify each intervention in detail. The pursuit of private interests does not have to be justified. Government has no business meddling unless it can show that the public interest requires it.

Nevertheless, misgivings may be felt about an interventionist theory. What is to prevent government abusing its authority? What was said in the last section about law may give some reassurance. A government which is subject to the rule of law is prevented from acting arbitrarily. But is this enough? Like everything human, government is fallible. Protection from stupidity and incompetence as well as from tyranny is desirable. This brings us to politics, which Crick rightly connected with representative government. That being so, an appropriate point of departure is with the idea of democracy.

4. Today there are two rival contenders for the title of democracy, the Western and the Communist. Modern Western democracy rests upon four main principles: the rule of law, representative government, constitutional opposition, and equality of citizenship. I do not say that in all Western democracies these principles are perfectly implemented: far from it. But I suggest that thoughtful adherents of Western democracy would agree that they are morally committed to them. Neither in theory nor in practice do Communists acknowledge any such commitment. They claim the title of democracy for something very different, wanting to have it for the sake of its favourable connotations. This is disingenuous because these favourable connotations arose in the first place from the theory and practice of Western democracy. In what follows therefore I shall equate 'democracy' with Western democracy. Let us look more closely at its main principles.[1]

A representative government is one which is drawn from and is accountable to, a wider citizen body, this being provided for by periodic elections. Hence the necessity for the rule of law: electoral procedure must be laid down by law and the government itself must be subject to the law. But if elections are to secure real accountability, there must be the opportunity for criticism and choice: hence the necessity for constitutional opposition. The composition of the citizen body is given by the fourth principle. It must be co-extensive with the whole adult population. That means universal suffrage and the equal right of all to be a candidate, to support or to oppose the government of the day.

The principle of constitutional opposition means what it says. Opposition must be within the limits of the law. You are free to criticize the government and to form or join parties which are opposed to it. But you are not free to undermine its authority to govern, not free to promote disobedience to it. It follows that there can be constitutional opposition and therefore democracy, only where the great majority of the population have a clear practical understanding of the difference between opposition and rebellion. But they must not only understand the difference. They must be able and willing to act on it, which means acknowledging the supremacy of law and eschewing all forms of revolutionary action.

[1] Cf. Milne, op. cit., Chapter 8 especially pp. 261–74.

Under the representative principle what the government is, or should be, accountable for is its work of identifying and promoting the public interest at home and the national interest abroad. Being fallible, its judgements about what needs to be done and how best to do it are always open to criticism. It is always in principle relevant to ask of any government measure: 'What are the particular conditions which it is intended to bring about?' 'Why are they in the public interest?' 'Is the measure the best way of achieving them?' Nor is this all. Economic considerations always impose limits upon what a government can do at any given time. The amount of human and material resources available is always finite. By no means all the conditions which are in the public interest can be brought about at once. This means that governing is inevitably always a matter of determining priorities.

Again, this is something which in principle is always open to criticism. The government can be called upon to explain and justify its particular order of priorities. The principle of constitutional opposition not only requires the government to permit such criticisms to be made but also morally obliges it to answer them. It must allow its answers to be subjected to comment and further criticism, and alternative policies to be advocated. The principle also requires that opposition should not only be constitutional but relevant: not merely opposition for the sake of opposing or winning the next election, but for the sake of bringing to light real government shortcomings and suggesting better policies.

This gives us the key to the concept of politics. It embraces everything which is relevant to implementing the representative principle and the principle of constitutional opposition. Elections are political occasions 'par excellence'. Every candidate when campaigning, every voter when voting, is acting politically. In an election, politics reaches a climax but it is not confined to elections. A government acts politically whenever it tries to explain, justify and defend its policies and to gain popular support. Opposition parties act politically whenever they question, criticize or comment upon government action, and when they advocate their own policies. Journalists, broadcasters and writers act politically whenever they express opinions about the merits or otherwise of the performance of both government and opposition.

More generally: if something is properly to be described as 'political', it must satisfy two conditions. The first is that it should have some bearing, direct or indirect, upon the work of identifying and promoting the public interest at home and the national interest abroad. The second, that it should at least potentially be controversial. Otherwise it will be of no significance in implementing the representative principle and the principle of constitutional opposition. The efficient enforcement of the criminal law is of the utmost relevance to the public interest. But that does not make it a political matter. On the other hand, proposals for penal reform about the merits of which opinions differ are a political matter.

A constitutional issue is likely to be, but need not necessarily be, political. When the American 'Founding Fathers' met in Philadelphia in 1787, they were grappling with political matters. They were drawing up a constitution which provided for representative government, albeit with a limited citizen body, and for constitutional opposition. Their proposals were controversial and had to be defended in the 'Federalist' papers. Where the form of government is representative, a constitutional amendment which extends the suffrage is political. It widens the range of persons from whom the government is drawn and to whom it is accountable, and is at least potentially controversial. The same is true of a constitutional amendment which either enacts a Bill of Rights, or makes changes in an existing one. Such an amendment affects what the government is accountable for, affects the grounds of relevant opposition, and again is at least potentially controversial.

On the other hand, a change in the rules of succession to the throne in a hereditary monarchy is a constitutional change which is not, as such, political. If the government is in the hands of the monarch and his appointees, it cannot affect the implementing of the representative principle and the principle of constitutional opposition because these principles are not being implemented at all.

A logical consequence of the concept of politics here presented is that there can be no politics properly so called unless the form of government is representative. Revolutionary movements against a despotism are not political. This may be objected to on linguistic grounds. It is surely odd to say that Lenin's activities in Czarist Russia were not political. Perhaps it is, but my concern is with concepts not merely with words. If by 'politics' is simply meant 'having something to do with government or the state', then the old Russian Social Democratic Party was political no less than the British Labour Party or the American Republican Party are political. But this blanket use of the term glosses over vital differences. When the form of government is not representative, there is no public forum in which the government can be held accountable for what it does. Politics can only take the form of intrigue and subversion. It is of the utmost importance to be clear about the difference between participating in the public forum and engaging in intrigue and subversion.

At the beginning of this essay, I said I was specially concerned with the question: 'How should we think of politics?' My answer is: as embracing everything relevant to implementing the representative principle and the principle of constitutional opposition; in short, in terms of the public forum. I am not saying that the words 'politics' and 'political' must not be used to refer to revolutionary movements, or to intrigue and subversion.[1] That would be to indulge in the pointless activity of linguistic legislation. But I am insisting on clarity of thought, on knowing what we are talking about, and on recognizing differences of substance.

In the last section, I said that the idea of the public interest is the relevant criterion for critically appraising government. This means that it is the perspective from which politics should be regarded. We have seen that the public interest has a rational basis and that it is essentially moral in character. Self-interest too has a rational basis. But we have seen that its perspective is morally defective compared with that of the public interest. The government is accountable for the public interest. Private interests and the public interest are not essentially complementary. When there is a conflict between them, on rational and moral grounds the public interest ought to have priority. Hence self-interest cannot be rationally justified as the perspective from which to regard politics. All the same, it may be urged that as a matter of empirical fact most people approach politics from the standpoint of their own individual self-interest. It is what voters think about when voting. Politicians appeal to it, or rather to the common self-interest of the greatest number when seeking votes.

No doubt there is a good deal of truth in this. But it does not invalidate the concept of politics presented here which, like the theory of government upon which it is based, is normative. To the extent that the public forum becomes an arena of competing private interests, politics degenerates and the proper work of government is less well done. That is not to say that the public interest will be entirely neglected. Although never completely identical, the perspectives of the public interest and of private interests overlap at many points. But politics properly so called is more than merely enlightened self-interest, and representative government can be good government only to the extent that this is appreciated and acted upon.

I criticized De Jouvenel for failing to provide a criterion for differentiating between political and other 'designs'. This gap is filled by the two conditions which must be satisfied before anything can be properly described as political. 'Instigation' and 'response' certainly play a large part in the activities falling under the concept of politics. But what is instigated and responded to must be relevant to implementing the representative principle and the principle of constitutional opposition.

As for Crick, his concept of politics lacks the perspective of the public interest. In his version of the representative principle, all that the

---

[1] In fact I think the etymology of the word 'politics' lends some support to the concept presented here. cf. Aristotle and what he discussed under that title in his *Politics*. But I cannot pursue this matter further here.

government is accountable for is survival. This makes the public forum an arena of competing private interests held in check only by prudential considerations. There is nothing specially political about conciliation and compromise. They are likely to be involved in getting people to co-operate for many purposes, including those properly described as political. Their importance in industrial relations is obvious. They are therefore relevant to the work of government, since it is in the public interest to foster co-operation 'in place of strife' in that sphere. But that is all. I am much closer to Crick, however, when it comes to what he defends politics against. This is because politics in terms of the public forum is for the most part threatened by the same enemies. But among the latter he cites democracy, having in mind democracy as 'majority rule'. His objections do not apply to democratic representative government as I have presented it here. But there are three matters about which something needs to be said and with which I will conclude this essay.

The first concerns the majority principle. Its role is confined to electoral procedure. Democratic government is fully developed representative government: not government by the majority, or according to the will of the majority; but in terms of the idea of the public interest, carried on by those who have gained most votes at the last election.

The second concerns the composition of the citizen body. Why extend it to the whole adult population? Why not confine it to those capable of the responsibilities of citizenship and hence of contributing positively to politics? To this, the short answer is that in the absence of any simple test of this capacity, it is wiser to open the citizen body to all, albeit at the risk of including many who are virtual passengers.

The third concerns two important pre-requisites for democracy, one social, the other cultural. The social pre-requisite is the absence of serious social conflict. The ersatz characteristic of the community must be minor. Democracy presupposes that differences over political issues do not run too deep, and that it does not matter too much who wins the next election. Where it does matter, as in an ersatz community divided along racial, religious or economic lines, there can be no real accountability of the government to the whole adult population. The cultural pre-requisite is a widespread well-developed tradition of discussion and criticism. People must be used to arguing and disagreeing without coming to blows. This presupposes the widespread recognition that to most questions there is more than one side and that those who are on the opposite side are not, for that reason, either knaves or fools.

These two prerequisites explain why democracy has taken root and lasted in only a few of the nations of the modern world. But for two main reasons, where you can get it, it is certainly worth having. One is negative, resting on prudential considerations. More than any other form of government, democracy takes account of and provides protection against human fallibility. It recognizes that no individual and no single group has a monopoly of wisdom or virtue. The other is positive, resting upon the recognition of human potentialities for constructive achievement. By extending the citizen body to the whole adult population, democracy opens the public forum to anyone who has anything to contribute to implementing the representative principle and the principle of constitutional opposition. To try to undermine it where it is a going concern, to resort to the politics of intrigue and subversion instead of the politics of the public forum, is to behave like a political Luddite.

Realism and Self-Interest as Political Themes

R. S. DOWNIE

I

It is often said that self-interest is the basic political motive; and it is in Machiavelli that we find one source of this view. Another source is in Hobbes, but there are important differences between the two thinkers. For, whereas Hobbes is concerned with the self-interest of *all men* and their salvation from its consequences in the establishment of political society with an absolute ruler, Machiavelli is concerned with various forms of the self-interest of the *prince* or *ruler*. But, although the theses of Machiavelli are different from those of Hobbes, both men contribute to what we might call the cynical strain in political philosophy. In this essay I want to draw attention to some of the many ambiguities and confusions in this strain, and to restate the case for the view that the aim of the ruler is 'interest', but in a way which will free it from its associations with wickedness which have delighted some commentators and distressed others.

II

An essential step in this analysis (and one worth taking for its own sake) is to eliminate a term which simply causes confusion in discussions of self-interest – realism. It is sometimes said that Machiavelli is a realist in his political theory, and his realism is contrasted with the idealism of other writers before and since his time. A distinguished example of the confusing use of the term 'realism' is to be found in the influential essay which forms the Introduction to Max Lerner's edition of *The Prince and the Discourses*.[1] Thus, Lerner writes of *The Prince*: 'Here we are in the presence of something little short of a revolution in

[1] Max Lerner, Introduction to *The Prince and the Discourses*. New York, Random House, 1950. The Introduction is also collected in a volume edited by De Lamar Jensen, *Machiavelli*. Boston, D. C. Heath and Co, 1960.

political thinking. The humanists who had written books about princes had written in the idealistic and scholastic medieval tradition; they were ridden by theology and metaphysics. Machiavelli rejected metaphysics, theology, idealism. The whole drift of his work is towards a political realism, unknown in the formal writing of his time' (p. xxxi). Again, Lerner writes: 'The Prince is part of the world's polemical literature because it places itself squarely in the ranks of realism. It brushes aside, with an impatience in which Machiavelli scarcely cares to conceal his disdain, the tender-mindedness of reformers and idealists' (p. xxxiv).

But although Lerner attaches great importance to what he is calling Machiavelli's 'realism', it is not clear exactly what phenomenon he has in mind. In the first place, he sometimes seems to be thinking of the logical status or category of Machiavelli's analyses. It sometimes seems, that is, that what Lerner and other commentators have found in Machiavelli and labelled 'realism', is an empirical (historical or sociological) analysis of political life. Machiavelli is a realist, according to this approach, because he describes how *in fact* princes behave. Just as Harvey simply recognized the circulation of the blood, Machiavelli (we are told) simply recognized the existence of certain phenomena of political life and examined them scientifically (p. xliii).

In the second place, Lerner sometimes seems to call Machiavelli a realist not only because he used an empirical method but also because of what he is thought to have found by using this method – namely, the phenomenon of power politics. It is said that Machiavelli, as an observer of human affairs, found that princes struggle desperately for power and have few scruples in the ruthless pursuit of their self-interested policies. It should be noted that this second thesis about realism is ambiguous, for it is not clear whether the claim is that the prince pursues power on his own behalf or on behalf of his state. Both claims have sometimes been made and can be found in Machiavelli's writings[1] and in Lerner's Introduction (pp. xliv, xlv). I shall later discuss the two claims, but in the meantime simply note that there is an empirical strain in political analysis to the effect that princes in fact pursue their own interests.

A third type of thesis about realism in political life is involved when Lerner says (p. xxxiv) that 'Machiavelli wrote a grammar of power, not only for the sixteenth century, but for the ages that followed.' Now the idea of a grammar is a normative one, for a grammar asserts what ought to be said or done. Developing the grammatical analogy, Lerner writes (p. xxxiv) that Machiavelli '... came close to setting down the imperatives by which men govern and are governed in political communities, whatever the epoch and whatever the governmental structure'.

[1] See Herbert Butterfield, *The Statecraft of Machiavelli* (London, Bell, 1940), pp. 108–10.

Now an empirical theme and a normative theme of the types described, although they ought to be distinguished, are not necessarily incompatible, because it might be said that the writer of a grammar first discovers what the customary usage is and then erects it as a norm. This is true of grammars of language and there is no reason why it should not be true also of a grammar of power. If *The Prince* is, as Lerner suggests (p. xxxv), a 'hard-bitten inquiry into how things actually get accomplished in a real political world', then it may not be inconsistent to claim that it is also a grammar telling the young politician how to get things accomplished. My point is not that the two are incompatible but that it is confusing to describe them both as 'realism'.

Incompatibility does appear, however, with the fourth type of thesis to be detected in the use of the term 'realism'. The fourth type of thesis is, surprisingly, a moral thesis. I say that this is surprising because Lerner himself contrasts sharply the moral (which he sometimes calls the 'idealistic') point of view with the 'realistic'. For example, he writes (p. xxxii) that Machiavelli had 'the daring to turn against the whole idealistic preoccupation of the humanists. He had the clear-eyed capacity to distinguish man as he ought to be and man as he actually is – between the ideal form of institutions and the pragmatic conditions under which they operate.' Again, he writes (p. xxxv) that 'There is in all of us, along with the ethical and normative strain, a strain of hard-headedness and of the acceptance of the framework of human passions and social reality within which we have to work'.

In these quotations, and elsewhere in his Introduction, Lerner seems to be contrasting the moral point of view in politics with the realistic. But in his concluding paragraph 'realism' appears once again, this time *within* the sphere of morality (described in this context not as 'idealism' or 'what ought to be' but as 'democratic values'). Thus, we are told that 'To be realistic about methods in the politics of a democracy at home does not mean that you throw away all scruples, or accept the superior force of "reason of state" . . . To be realistic about the massing of power abroad in the economic and ideological struggle . . . does not mean that you abandon the struggle for peace . . . We may yet find that an effective pursuit of democratic values is possible within the scope of a strong social-welfare state and an unsentimental realism about human motives.'

In Lerner's Introduction, then, we find four rather different points of view all being described as 'realistic'. This is confusing. The various theses in the Introduction all merit discussion, but should not be prejudged by the use of the emotive word 'realistic'. In particular, the earlier contrast between the moral point of view in politics (shrugged off as 'idealism') and realism ('how things actually get accomplished in a real political world') seems unfortunate in view of the fact that the moral point of view ('democratic values') is finally brought back as 'humanist realism'. To make these criticisms of Lerner's Introduction, of course, is not to decry it in other respects, for it is a stimulating piece of writing which provides many excellent details of Machiavelli's general approach to politics, and sets it in its historical context. But it is to say that some of the substantial issues of the relation between morality and politics with which Machiavelli is concerned require to be distinguished one from another. The general conclusion I shall later suggest is not, I believe, so very different from that which Lerner himself reaches, but I shall argue for it without using the word 'realism'.

III

The first thesis I shall consider is that rulers always in fact pursue their own interests in political life. Let us call this thesis A(i). It is undeniable that this view is to be found in the layman's coffee-room discussions of politics, and that it is to be found also in some theoretical writings, perhaps not always clearly distinguished from other theses.

Let us put the thesis into a more general context. We might say that men try to explain their relationship to a ruler by invoking some more familiar type of relationship. For example, some theorists use the analogy of the parent and the child or the guardian and the ward. The ruler is said to exercise his power with the same sort of justification as a parent might have for exercising power or authority over a child. This analogy is common in 'divine right' theories of government, and is reflected in the political practice of some of the 'enlightened despots' of the eighteenth century. It has often been criticized, but undoubtedly it reflects in its various forms some deep-rooted desire in the human mind to be 'looked after'.

A second sort of analogy which has often been invoked is that of the legal contract or promise. The subjects of a state are thought to give up some rights in return for which the ruler rules for their advantage. Once again, we can find in the analogy an attempt to make sense of the existence of government or of a ruler by invoking a familiar idea which is widely acceptable – that one has in some indirect sense consented to or voluntarily entered into the peculiar relationship of ruler and ruled.

Now these two approaches, whatever their difficulties (and they are many and notorious), have in common the assumption that the relationship between ruler and ruled is at bottom justifiable and rational. But there is often to be found side by side with such theories a much more cynical type of analogy – that of the farmer and his livestock. We find this analogy expressed, for example, in the *Republic*. Thrasymachus rejects as naïve the view that the ruler rules for the good of his subjects.

According to him the ruler is like a shepherd who fattens the sheep for the good of the shepherd. And from the time of Plato there is always to be found in political writing the theme of the exploitation for personal advantage of the subjects by the ruler. This is the background to thesis A(i).

Whatever plausibility this thesis may have had as an interpretation of the policies of the absolute ruler of a primitive community – and even here there are difficulties, for primitive communities have their own systems of checks and balances – it is not plausible as an interpretation of the policies of a ruler in the modern bureaucratic state. In the modern bureaucratic state, official business is conducted in terms of procedural regulations. There is a strict hierarchy of authority, and each official within the hierarchy is limited to a specific type of task and has the necessary authority to carry it out, for the most part using written documents. It is true that for certain purposes we might need to distinguish the role of the administrator – the civil servant – from that of the politician, but the influence of bureaucracy is all-pervasive in the modern state. The result is that the actions of a ruler are more open to public scrutiny than they would be in some avocational form of government, and hence the possibility of the exploitation of the ruled for the personal material benefit of the ruler is limited (although no doubt it still exists).

By drawing attention to the limitations on personal aggrandisement which a bureaucratic system brings with it, I have tried to dilute the strength of A(i). But this is to use an argument with only contingent force, whereas a radical conceptual argument can be deployed if we draw a distinction which exponents of A(i) do not always notice. The distinction is between the *motive* a person might have for seeking a certain office or seeking a certain job, and the *nature of his actions* in the office or in doing the job. It may well be the case that it is self-interest in some form which leads a person to seek a certain office. This may be the self-interest of someone who wants a large salary or it may be a more complex form of self-interest, such as the desire for fame, honour, a life-peerage, etc. But it does not follow from the fact that self-interest in some form leads a person to seek or retain a certain office that his actions in the office will be self-interested. Indeed, it may well be that his desire to succeed in the office will lead him to be self-sacrificial and to work in it for the good of others. Hence, the actions performed in the office may be as ideally they should be, although the underlying motive is vainglory. I believe that failure to draw this distinction is an important theoretical reason why A(i) is so often asserted.

Another reason is simply a persistent practical attitude of cynicism. The cynicism, moreover, can take a fresh form in new historical situations, and is quite compatible with the existence of the bureaucratic state. It has been said, for example, that politicians are sometimes encouraged by industrialists to prolong or begin wars or to create unemployment, and that the industrialists have the means to ensure that the interests of the politicians are furthered in some direct or indirect way. This attitude of cynicism obviously has some justification and it will persist as long as there is political society, but it does not justify the adoption of A(i) as an adequate account of the relationship between ruler and ruled.

There is another thesis A(ii) which in many respects resembles A(i): that a ruler always pursues the interests of a dominant class (as distinct from his own personal interests). It is difficult to make sense of this thesis independently of A(i). If the dominant class is a very small one – a ruling clique, such as a royal household – then it is better thought of as an extension of A(i), and it will have the same merits and defects as A(i). But if the class concerned is very large – the middle and upper classes, say – then it becomes a different type of thesis. It becomes the thesis B, that the ruler rules in the interests of some form of political party which represents the interests of a section of the community. Let us consider B.

The point about B which is immediately significant, and distinguishes it from the first sort of thesis, is that it would not normally be held as a *de facto* but as a *de iure* thesis. The point is that members of political parties characteristically hold that the policies and general philosophy of their parties are in the interests of the whole continuing community. It is true that party members may admit that their policies are in the present interests of, say, the working class or the middle class, but they would also hold that the expansion and prosperity of that section of the community is in the best interests of the whole historical community. Now whereas it is not a rational position to hold theses A(i) or A(ii) in a normative form – to assert that a ruler *ought* to pursue his own interests or those of a small group – it is a rational position to hold that a ruler ought to pursue the interests of a political party, if it is also assumed (and this is built into the conception of a political party) that furthering its interests is *ipso facto* furthering those of the whole community. Hence, we have now a position to discuss which is not sociological (or cynical) but normative in some sense: that the ruler ought to further the interests of the whole community (perhaps by means of party politics). Let us call this thesis C.

IV

I have said that thesis C is in some sense normative, but what is the sense? What sort of 'ought' is it when it is said that the ruler ought to further the interests of the whole community?

One answer to this question might be that the 'ought' is definitional. In that case, 'Rulers ought to further the interests of the community they rule' would be necessarily true, an analytic statement similar to 'Farmers ought to cultivate the ground they farm' or 'Knives ought to cut.'

There is a certain plausibility in taking this line, because it seems to obviate the embarrassment of moral judgements and settles the issue in a clear-cut way. It is not a satisfactory solution, however, and the difficulty in it emerges if we inquire what we can legitimately say about the ruler who does not rule in the interests of his subjects. We can say that he is not a good ruler, but hardly that he is not a ruler at all. This is quite a different case from that of the farmer, who, if he never cultivates the ground, tends his animals, etc., is not a farmer at all, rather than simply not a good farmer. A farmer must aim at certain specifiable ends to be a farmer, just as a knife must be able to do certain specifiable things to be a knife. What, then, does a ruler have to do to be a ruler?

The question must be rejected, for it is misleading. To give an account of what it is to be a ruler is to refer not to what the man happens to do, but rather to the *authorization* for his actions. A man can be said to be a ruler if what he does is authorized by certain procedures established in his society. The point is that in any society there are rules which define the offices of government. These rules are different from the rules, legal or moral, which direct the conduct of the members of the community in their normal activities, for they lay down the procedures to be invoked for a man to be empowered or enabled to do certain things such as pass judgements, arrest or impose taxes. We can call these the constitutional rules of the society. Now if someone rightfully acts according to the relevant constitutional procedures of the society then he is a ruler, whether or not what he does is in the interests of the members of the community.

As an objection to this account of what it is to be a ruler it can be maintained that an invader might seize power without going through the constitutional procedures. The reply is that we must distinguish what it is to *be* a ruler from what it is to *become* a ruler. Before a man can truly be said to *be* a ruler he must make use of the relevant constitutional or other established procedures. This is necessary for the ordinary business of governing, otherwise no one will know whose orders he ought to obey; for even if the ruler is an invader, people will still need some *legal* distinction between the invader's henchmen and ordinary criminals. Normally a man will also *become* a ruler according to constitutional procedures, but occasionally there may be a revolution or an invasion and a man may seize power. When that happens he may be said to be a ruler *de facto* and perhaps he will be opposed by a ruler *de iure* who is in exile.

But if he continues to rule *de facto* then he will in course of time be recognized as the new ruler *de iure*. And this is likely to happen the sooner if when he is the ruler *de facto* he acts as far as he can according to the pre-invasion constitutional procedures. It is to constitutional procedures, then, that we must look for definitions of what it is to be a ruler, rather than to the ends, such as the interests of subjects, which a ruler may or may not pursue.

If, then, the thesis, that rulers ought to seek the interests of their subjects, is not *a priori* analytic, is it *a posteriori* synthetic? In other words, is it the case that rulers ought to further the interests of their subjects lest various contingent things may befall them which they would not desire, such as being ejected from power? If this is the justification for the thesis, then it is in fact a hypothetical imperative, a hint that might be found in a handbook for the complete ruler. 'Rulers who wish to stay in power ought to arrange annual ceremonial displays, and they ought to seek the interests of their subjects.' Such an account, while it certainly does reflect an important truth, does not do justice to the thesis. Many rulers who have attempted to further the interests of their subjects have been successful rulers, but others have been overthrown; and others again, (such as Louis XIV) who have not been conspicuous for their concern for the interests of their subjects, have not been overthrown.

If, then, the thesis that rulers ought to pursue the interests of their subjects is not a definition (*a priori* analytic) and it is not based on a report or a recipe (*a posteriori* synthetic), then it must be a moral judgement (*a priori* synthetic). It is a moral judgement which is so commonly made that it is easy to mistake it for a definition. We need not deny that a ruler who does not attempt to follow the precept is running a grave risk of being removed from power by his subjects or by another ruler, but the reason why he ought to pursue the interests of his subjects is simply that this is the only sort of policy which is morally defensible from one who is in the office of ruler.

It is interesting to note that Plato is confused over the sense in which a ruler ought to pursue the interests of his subjects. In meeting the arguments of Thrasymachus he uses what is known as the '*techne* argument'. A *techne* is a skill or craft, and Plato assumes that every *techne* furthers only one specific end peculiar to itself. Thus the carpenter qua carpenter is concerned with making things out of wood, and the ruler qua ruler is concerned with furthering the interests of his subjects. As a concession to Thrasymachus, Socrates admits that a craft or art may have attached to it the separate *techne* of wage-earning, and hence while the doctor qua doctor is concerned to heal the sick, he may qua wage-earner make some money out of it. Likewise the ruler qua ruler is concerned to further the interests of his subjects, but he may also qua wage-earner make a profit.

Now Plato is fundamentally confused in his use of the *techne* argument here. In the first place, while it may or may not be true that the jobs of doctor or musician are to be defined in terms of certain skills directed towards certain ends, we have already seen that this is not true of a ruler. A ruler is not likely to survive long without certain skills, and I have pointed out that it is advisable for him to direct these skills towards the end of the welfare of his subjects; but it is not correct to define 'being a ruler' in terms of the possession of these skills or the pursuit of these ends. To be a ruler is to be a person or group empowered by the constitutional rules of the society to take certain decisions, initiate certain policies, etc. Plato may be correct in suggesting that wage-earning (or profiteering) as such is something essentially separate from ruling, although it may be contingently connected with it; but it does not follow that we can analyse what it is to be a ruler in terms of the skilful pursuit of the interests of those being ruled.

In the second place, there is a more general confusion which is attached to many of the uses to which Plato (and Aristotle for that matter) put the *techne* argument. To say, 'The object of craft X is end Y' – 'The object of horsemanship is to win in battle' – is to confuse the three types of thesis we have distinguished above. It is to confuse the definition of a craft or activity, what the craft or activity happens at a certain historical moment to be used for, and what the craft or activity ought (morally) to be used for. Thus, it may have been the case in Plato's day that the point of practising horsemanship was to help to win victories, but it does not follow that horsemanship can be defined in these terms or that this morally ought to be the object of it. In a similar way, it may be the case that rulers morally ought to pursue the interests of their subjects, but this moral judgement cannot be validated by an appeal to what rulers in fact do to survive or by pretending that it is a definition. The conclusion of this section, then, is that thesis C is a straightforward moral judgement.

V

The question we must now consider is whether it is a moral judgement with which Machiavelli would disagree. On the face of it, it might seem that he need not disagree with it. There are contexts when he does not distinguish thesis C from A(i) or A(ii), but his stress in *The Discourses* on the themes of republicanism, democracy, national unity and so on, suggests that he had his own definite ideas of what the interest of the members of a state consists of, and that he thought it was the bounden duty of the ruler to further these. Machiavelli's notoriety stems from his view of the *means* whereby he thought such ends could most effectively be furthered. His characteristic contribution to the history of political thought and his continuing influence are connected with the *techniques* which he advocated. The question I wish to raise is whether there is any incompatibility between accepting thesis C – the moral judgement that a ruler ought to pursue the interests of his subjects – and accepting the sort of account which Machiavelli provided of the means of furthering such an end.

Let us first consider the matter as it applies to the domestic policies of a ruler. Is it the case that there is any inconsistency between pursuing the interests of the subjects and using means to do this which may involve deceit? In discussing this question it is very easy to slip back into arguments directed more at thesis A(i). For it is often and plausibly said that professional politicians are always reluctant to give up power and stick at nothing to retain it. Now this view does not really raise any special theoretical problems. The issues are the same as those involved when a person is anxious to retain a job of a non-political kind, and is unscrupulous in the claims he makes about himself and his achievements in order to do so.

There may, of course, be one psychological factor which results in a politician being more unscrupulous than a professional or business man in the means he adopts to retain his job: his belief that only he or his party can truly serve the interests of the people. This belief, which may be held to a pathological extent, focuses attention on C – that a ruler ought to pursue the interests of his subjects – which it presupposes. Let us therefore consider whether there is any inconsistency in domestic policies between C and Machiavellian techniques.

It might be said that, far from there being an incompatibility, Machiavellian techniques are definitely required to persuade the electorate to accept certain policies. To bring this out, consider first the nature of the 'public' whose interests are to be furthered by the ruler. The 'public interest' is not that of any given group of individuals who happen to make up part of the membership of a society. It is not even that of the majority of the members of a society at a given time. The 'public interest' which is being furthered is that of the whole continuing social community. To say this, of course, is not to say that there is a mysterious spirit 'the public' over and above the individuals who make up the public, but it is to say that the interest of the public, or of the continuing community, requires the continued existence and prosperity of institutions such as banks, insurance companies, schools and organizations of all kinds, as well as various long-term policies such as town and country planning, re-afforestation, slum clearance and so on, and the nature of these institutions and policies cannot be adequately analysed in terms of the interests of any group of actual individuals. Now if this, as far as it goes, is a true account of 'public interest', then a ruler will be required to persuade his subjects to accept policies which may not be in their own immediate interests. And it is at this point that the use of Machiavellian techniques may be necessary to gild the political pill. Are we then conceding that Machiavellianism is a legitimate means?

If we are, we are doing so only after three fundamental qualifications have been made. The first is that there need be nothing morally reprehensible about gilding the pill. Any salesman is entitled to describe his products in the most favourable way he can, and there is no reason why the techniques of the salesman and the public relations expert should not be put to political service. If this technique goes beyond certain limits, however, we then have a different situation, as when a salesman does not simply describe his wares as favourably as he can but actually makes false claims about them. Is the deliberate making of false claims compatible with thesis C? The answer to this question takes us to the second point.

Sometimes it may be quite legitimate for a politician to tell a deliberate lie about his policies. For example, let us suppose that a Prime Minister is unfortunately put in the position whereby he must answer a question about his government's intentions to devalue. To tell the truth on such an occasion may quite defeat the object of devaluation, and to say nothing may be as revealing as to tell the truth. On such an occasion a politician will surely be committed by his acceptance of C to tell a lie. Such situations will be extremely rare and a skilful politician will avoid as far as he can being placed in them. For (and this is the main substance of the second point) it is a contingent truth that frequent dishonesty or general trickery is not only against a politician's own individual interest – he is liable to be exposed by his opponents – it is also against the public interest. It is bad for the political health of a community if political argument is systematically replaced by public relations. Even if the general lines of a ruler's policies are in the public interest, there will be a general atmosphere of distrust or apathy which is a breeding-ground for discontent and division in a community. The second point, then, is that whereas there may be a (very) few occasions when a straightforward lie is morally imperative, the use of such means as a continuing technique of government is likely to be counter-productive. This (I am claiming) is a contingent truth about politics which sets strict limits to subtle techniques.

But the limits set by the second argument are only contingent ones. It might be said that a skilful manipulator could escape detection. Are there any *a priori* or necessary limits to Machiavellian techniques which are implied by C? An answer to this question (at least as far as domestic policy is concerned) may be obtained if we look more closely at the conception of ends and means. Are political means connected only contingently with political ends? This leads to the third point.

There are two main sorts of means/end relationship. In the first, the means are instrumental to the end, but have no part in the end when it has been brought about. For example, a paint brush is an instrumental means to the painting of a picture, but it has no place in the finished picture (unless in very advanced modern art!). On the other hand, some means are an integral part of the end and are factors which determine the final nature of the end. For example, we might say (to continue the analogy from painting) that certain shapes on the canvas are means to the completed picture. Means of this second sort we might call 'component means' and they differ from instrumental means in that they are essentially connected with the end as determining features.

Applying the distinction between instrumental or contingent means and component or essential means to the problem of political techniques, we can say that political techniques are component means in that they determine the nature of the political end produced. This is true in the sense that political techniques affect the nature of a political tradition, which in turn affects what can actually be accomplished politically. Political trickery is not something which when started can easily be stopped. Further intrigues are necessary to maintain the advantages gained, and further tricks must be devised by the opponents of the policies. The result is instability and general social uncertainty, which sometimes only a revolution can alter.

The conclusion which this suggests, then, is that Machiavellian means, which may seem compatible with the political ends suggested by C, are really incompatible with it. The reason is not simply that they *may* be unsuccessful as instrumental means to the ends, but that they *must* be unsuccessful since they are component means which enter into the political end and determine its nature.

If we turn now to the foreign affairs of a country, it is not obvious how far the same sorts of argument apply. The reason is that, whereas in domestic matters it is clearly in the interests of the subjects that the ruler should preserve the integrity of a tradition of political debate, it is not obvious that similar considerations apply in foreign policy. But let us consider how far they do.

Thesis C is to the effect that a ruler morally ought to further the interests of his subjects. But this does not mean that he is obliged to further the interests of the subjects of any other state. On the contrary, it may be that he should further the interests of his own subjects even at the expense of those of other states. This seems to imply that in international relations morality has no place, either in respect of the ends pursued or in respect of the means whereby they are pursued. Does this suggest that we have uncovered the real context for Machiavellianism?

Let us take first the question of means, which was the only question relevant in our discussion of domestic policy. Similar considerations are applicable to the foreign policy of a ruler. Thus sometimes, though very rarely, duplicity, the threat of naked power or even the use of it, may be justifiable. But such expedients must very rarely be good policy. Duplicity is just as apt to rebound in international affairs as in personal relationships, and wars are economically crippling. Thus, as a contingent instrumental means, Machiavellian techniques seem to have severe limitations in the international field. But can they be ruled out essentially as being also component means which would therefore create an international situation inimical to C? The answer is that they can, and for reasons not unlike the ones which applied to domestic policy. The continued interests of a state depend on good international relations, and they in turn depend on traditions of international diplomacy. And where these are not present then the interests of the state necessarily suffer.

An analogy with a trustee may be helpful here. A trustee is morally obliged to further, as far as he can, the interests of the trust he is representing, but it does not follow from this that he ought to use unscrupulous means when he tries to further the interests of the trust. In a similar way, a ruler is a trustee of the national interest, but it does not follow that he ought to depart from accepted standards of international diplomacy to be so. On the contrary, he is obliged to preserve and maintain these standards and to encourage other rulers to act likewise, because the nature of these standards will essentially affect what he can achieve as a trustee. To argue in this way is to say that Machiavellianism is ruled out as a *technique* of international negotiations by thesis C.

Does C have any implications for the pursuit of *ends* in the international field? It does, in two respects. First of all, it is a commonplace of economics that nations are increasingly interdependent and that economic difficulties in one state affect other states. Moreover, it is thought to be politically important for nations to have spheres of interest in which they can to a greater or lesser extent influence the policies of other states. These facts constitute grounds which justify the use of the national resources of one state to aid those of a less developed state. It may be said to this that such action exemplifies not morality but national self-interest. Well, that may be so, but we should avoid being too hard on ourselves over it. Whatever the national motivation which may lead one state to help a less developed one (and it certainly happens) this is probably the morally right course anyway. Hence, we can say that an enlightened conception of national interest will lead a ruler to pursue in the international field ends which in any case morality would require.

Once again an analogy with a trustee may be helpful. A trustee has a fair amount of discretion about his use of the trust. If he regards it as suitable he may use the funds of the trust for some purpose with which he believes the benefactors would have sympathy. And in a similar way a ruler may make limited use of national resources for certain purposes with which public opinion in his state might be thought to have some sympathy – as in the provision of aid to the victims of serious disasters in other less wealthy states, the provision of educational resources, etc. Of course, the cynical may see in this some disguised furthering of national self-interest. But we need not deny this, and indeed it is not clear what sort of considerations could enable this sort of ambiguity to be resolved. The motives of actual politicians? If so, there would be evidence for the view that some at least may have the highest humanitarian motives. But we need not argue the toss on this matter, for it is sufficient to point out that if this is the pursuit of national interest, it must surely be national interest interpreted in a very wide and enlightened way.

The conclusion then is that acceptance of C rules out Machiavellian means in both domestic and foreign policy, and that pursuit of national interest is quite compatible with, or may even imply, the limited pursuit of the interests of other states in the international field.

The Distinction between Moderation and Extremism

R. N. BERKI

'Moderation' and 'extremism' are emotion-laden words which almost defy straight definitions. In general usage, 'moderation' may stand for caution, circumspection, restraint, self-discipline, or a particular way of satisfying one's desires (as in doing something 'in moderation'). 'Extremism' usually means doing something in excess, or pushing something to its utmost limit, to have recourse to the last, ultimate method available. In politics the field of possible meanings is narrower, and there are a number of specific difficulties. 'Moderation', like 'democracy', is a term most often used in praise and approval. 'Extremism', like 'totalitarianism', is generally used in condemnation, though here, as everywhere else, the self-avowed extremism of such figures as Malcolm X, Barry Goldwater and Jean-Paul Sartre, provides exceptions to the rule. Another difficulty is that moderation and extremism, as imputed features of political movements or the behaviour of political actors, cut across party labels and ideologies. One can be a 'moderate' socialist or conservative, or an 'extremist' in the pursuit of almost any political end, left, right or centre.

However, moderation and extremism in politics do not merely reflect various intensities of commitments. Extremism is not just hotheadedness or inconsiderateness. Moderation is not the same as lukewarmness or timidity. They can also, and more profitably, be viewed as different logical types of commitment to which rules of internal consistency are applicable. In this essay an attempt will be made to draw sketches of moderation and extremism from this point of view.[1]

[1] Many writers on politics and ethics, of course, have drawn distinctions similar to the ones made here, without using the terms 'moderation' and 'extremism'. Some relevant and interesting arguments can be found, for example, in Max Weber's essay, 'Politics as a Vocation' (*From Max Weber: Essays in Sociology*, ed. by H. H. Gerth and C. Wright Mills. London, 1948); in Bertrand

THE DISTINCTION BETWEEN MODERATION AND EXTREMISM

We can, perhaps, start by defining moderation and extremism in politics along these lines: moderation is the acceptance of moral limits in the choice of means to achieve a political end, while extremism is the absence of such an acceptance. This seems, indeed, a correct approximation, but it does not go far enough. Somebody might be aware of and ready to accept limitations in his choice of means, but if his conception of morality is an off-beat one, he would be more likely labelled an eccentric, or a crank, but not a moderate. Similarly, lack of moral scruples in the choice of means would signify a cynic or (popularly but erroneously) a Machiavellian, but not always and necessarily an extremist. The presence or absence of 'moral limits' is undoubtedly the key to an understanding of the distinction between extremism and moderation, but it is necessary to endow the notion of 'moral limits' with a more determinate content. One can then perhaps amend the above definitions in the following way: moderation in politics means the voluntary and conscious resolution to confine oneself to such means in the pursuit of a political end as are compatible with generally accepted basic moral notions and the underlying political traditions of one's society; extremism means the consistent advocacy and employment of means that are incompatible with moral notions and political traditions.

It would be tempting, but wrong to conceive of the relevant 'basic moral notions' in a relativistic manner. It is not the case that moderation or extremism is measured in terms of values accepted within isolated communities or subcultures, but rejected by organized society at large. A member of Cosa Nostra would not be called an 'extremist' by anybody, and last of all by his bosses and colleagues, if he attempted to settle a score by prayer or persuasion instead of using his gun. Even in subcultures where a number of 'generally accepted moral notions' are held in ridicule, the moderate and the extremist are defined still by reference to underlying norms common to the whole of civilization.

It appears, then, that moderation and extremism turn on 'means' as opposed to 'ends', on *how* a political activist goes about pursuing his goal, and not on *what* he wants to achieve. But there is a problem. Strictly speaking, it is nearly always incorrect to apply moral judgements to means or methods, in isolation from the ends they purport to serve. A simple (and trivial) example could illustrate this point. Suppose a

---

Russell's *Human Society in Ethics and Politics* (London, 1954); and in R. M. Hare's *Freedom and Reason* (Oxford, 1963). The antitheses between an 'ethic of responsibility' and an 'ethic of ultimate ends' (Weber); between the 'scientific attitude' and 'dogmatism' (Russell); and between 'liberalism' and 'fanaticism' (Hare) have all, in their various ways, influenced the direction the present essay has taken. Their inspiration, perhaps it should be made clear, has often been of a negative character.

student, who wants badly to pass his examinations, considers that prima facie 'cheating' is a method that might just enable him to attain this end. Now the question is: what possible reasons could he have which would induce him to refrain from employing this method? There are two alternatives. Either he might come to the conclusion, having considered the matter carefully, that cheating would almost certainly lead to being found out by the examiners, and to being disqualified. This, clearly, is an empirical, technical criticism of the means, and it has nothing to do with morals. When means are said in this way to 'cancel out' their ends, the argument is reduced to a tautology: some means are inappropriate to a given end, because they will not achieve that end. Some means, in other words, turn out to be no means at all. (The Marxist rejection of political assassination as a means to achieve the revolution in the nineteenth century was based on technical considerations of an essentially similar kind.)

The other alternative for the student in our example is to decide not to resort to cheating because he thinks that 'cheating is wrong'. Here we certainly have a moral judgement, but does it really pertain to the 'means' as opposed to the 'end'? Only in one case does it pertain to the means: if the person subscribing to this moral prohibition seriously holds that 'cheating is wrong' always and everywhere, in all situations and circumstances. But this position – it can be called 'moral absolutism' – cannot be consistently held in politics, as I shall try to show later. (Moral absolutism, for that matter, is incompatible with most areas of practical morality – but this wider issue is irrelevant here.) However, if the student in our example succeeds in avoiding the trap of moral absolutism, the only other way in which he can adopt a moral stance *vis à vis* his predicament is by concretizing his moral judgement, that is, shifting his attention from means to ends. The relevant and valid moral rule in the present case will then be 'passing examinations by cheating is wrong', and not the abstract 'cheating is wrong'.

But why should this position be taken in the first place? There may be all sorts of reasons for adopting it, such as wanting to remain an 'honest man', or to have a clear conscience, or to be able to look friends in the face, and so on. The essential point about these reasons is that they are all concerned with ends, and all have their basis in the recognition that there is a plurality of ends and that ends are mutually self-limiting. In this particular example, what provides the moral basis for the student's rejection of the method of cheating is his recognition that the original, single end, passing his examination, does not override other and possibly more important ends he may have. Ends have to coexist with one another. Now, in a nutshell, we have here the essential ingredients for drawing the distinction between moderation and extremism. Moderation presupposes an awareness of the plurality and mutual limitation of ends, while extremism is the practical consequence of an agent's fastening on to one single, overriding end. In politics, of course, there are complications, both conceptual and existential, that may confuse the issues. Let us therefore see what 'ends' and 'means' might signify in a proper political context.

Political ends are conceptualizations, or mental pictures, of future states of affairs which their advocates – philosophers, propagandists, leaders and rank-and-file activists – look upon as both desirable and capable of realization. Political ends, in order to be intelligible and relevant to political action, have to be more limited and more circumscribed than are perennial and vacuous dreams about the 'good society' or 'universal happiness'. At the same time, however, they have also to be larger and more rounded than single policy-objectives, such as winning elections or fighting campaigns. Ends in politics are very much like war aims, as distinguished both from battle plans and from ultimate goals in life. They are particular definitions or articulations of the good society and universal happiness. To take as our illustrations three rather well-known ideologies of recent times: socialism, liberalism and racialism all in their separate ways embody political ends which depict desirable states of affairs in society. The socialist political end might be defined as a society without class distinctions and exploitation, a human community based on love, co-operation and mutual understanding. The liberal end appears as a society of unfettered individual advancement under the rule of law, the full use of human capabilities in the service of private improvements, a world where equality is everybody's starting-point, but inequality is everybody's aim. The racialist end could be seen as a world of homogeneous racial units where nations or races are related to one another through force and hegemony, and where (as in the Nazi variety) nations are united internally around dictatorial leaders. Now the essential point to make about political ends here is that although they are subject to *moral* criticism, they are not in themselves subject to moral criticism in terms of moderation and extremism.

What we have considered so far is only the *empirical* dimension of political ends, that is, the various concrete empirical features attributed to future states of society by people who are committed to work for their realization. This means that we have taken these ends in isolation, in the abstract, independently of what kind of relationship they might have to any political writer's or activist's conception of *existing* society. But not even the most fanatical Nazi activist could be properly described as an 'extremist' on account merely of what he sees as the good society. Not even the most humane and benign liberal can be called a 'moderate' by virtue only of the kind of future society he wants to see realized.

Something more is needed than empirical characteristics in our understanding of the nature of political ends, if we are to make sense of the distinction between extremism and moderation. What we want is a scale on which to measure (or at least to appreciate) the varying relationship in which political ends might stand to existing societies. A brief consideration of 'means' usually resorted to in the pursuit of political ends will, it is hoped, lead us on to an understanding of the relevant, but as yet uncharted, dimension of political ends.

Means can be conveniently graded according to the relative emphasis they place on the *end* to be achieved, at the expense of the *hindrances* to the end, or the other way round, on the obstacles standing in the way of a political activist's goal, at the expense of the goal itself. On the whole, it seems reasonable to argue that the greater emphasis laid on hindrances as opposed to the end itself, will result in the 'means' in question being a better indication as to the extremism or moderation of the political movement or activist involved.

The first category of means to receive our attention here is *integral* means. These are called such by many writers, because they stand in a relationship of logical implication to the ends they are supposed to serve. They are, in other words, considered by their advocates to be essential both to the achievement and to the maintenance of a certain kind of society. Integral means, indeed, are parts of the definition of their ends, and can hence be regarded as subordinate ends themselves. Examples are easy to find. In the case of the political end of socialism, persuasion by example, by actual demonstration of the superiority of a certain way of life over others, can be taken as an integral means. In the case of liberalism, the securing of majority votes in legal assemblies for the purpose of initiating policy changes is an example of the employment of integral means. In the case of racialism, 'scientific' research aimed at the breeding of racially pure specimens of human beings is also an integral means. Now it is quite clear that the employment or otherwise of integral means in the pursuit of any political end (excepting the megalomaniac dreams of madmen) is not a useful pointer to the putative extremism or moderation of the movement or activists involved. This is because integral means, by definition, must assume that the end is in the process of being fully realized, that there are virtually no obstacles separating an undesirable present from a desirable future.

Now no political end can be the literal advocacy of a kind of Hobbesian state of nature, envisaging and working towards a permanently unsettled, murderous, violent world. Though political ends do not converge (except on the level of empty platitudes), they are all the same in respect of their acknowledgement of certain generally accepted basic moral notions. Hence means which contain reference *merely* to ends, to the accomplished 'good societies' of the future, must necessarily entail the acceptance of certain moral limits. It would, therefore, be by and large true to say that the employment of integral means entails moderation. But the converse cannot be asserted. No political activists or movements can always (or even predominantly) confine themselves to the use of integral means. Usually there will be found difficulties of a mundane, empirical character. Many political ends are such that they cannot be achieved by integral means alone.

Thus we move on to the second category which we can call *contingent* means. These are means seen by people who urge their employment in political action as being empirically necessary to the achievement of the end they pursue, but which are at the same time logically independent of both the achievement and the maintenance of the end. A great many people (understandably) would feel uneasy about contingent means, and indeed, certain varieties of moral absolutism would declare an implacable opposition to their employment.[1] However, in the real world of politics contingent means are and have to be used by all and sundry, and practically all the time. It would be indeed very difficult to put our finger on more than a tiny handful of political changes in the course of our history that have been accomplished without recourse to contingent means. And quite apart from the difficulties involved with 'realization' – it will be agreed that to bring something into being is a more intricate operation than to maintain a going concern – contingent means have an important function in ensuring the survival of established and quite respectable political ends, such as the liberal-democratic societies of the Western world. For example, it is not necessary for liberalism to *be* liberalism to have recourse to such methods in government as preventive detention or the political branch of the police. These and similar methods, however, become necessary in an empirical context, once attention is paid to the end *as well as* to hindrances to the end's full realization.

Contingent means are those that will be often referred to by apologists of the *status quo* (any kind of *status quo*) as 'regrettable' and 'lamentable', but none the less 'warranted' by the prevailing situation. The point is, of course, that contingent means *are* warranted in most cases, that is,

[1] Aldous Huxley's once famous book, *Ends and Means* (London, 1937), comes fairly close to the attitude which is here labelled 'moral absolutism'. The author of a not-so-famous critique of Huxley, however, gave the appropriate reply to all arguments of this type: 'The condition of attaining an end, the good, is . . . the employment of means capable of coping with that which is not good. The formula that good means alone can lead to good ends ignores the obvious truth that, in the very nature of the case, means must deal with or relate to that which is external to the end and hence not good.' K. S. Shelvankar, *Ends are Means* (London, 1938), p. 37.

justifiable in terms of political ends that have to be fought for in a stubborn, imperfect world, not allowing their realization to the full. This means that the justification of contingent means requires *also* moral criteria that do not presuppose that the bright future is here: moral criteria which therefore are in a sense more basic and wider in application than the political ends and contingent means which they are brought in to justify.

Is it, then, the case that the employment of contingent means marks off extremists from moderates? Not quite. Both extremism and moderation are compatible with the use of contingent means, and in actual fact the latter is more likely to go with moderation than with extremism. This is because (to anticipate our argument) contingent means presuppose that the end is *limited*. This is quite obvious. If any method can be logically independent of the end it serves, it means that the end in question is something less than an all-embracing one: a 'good society' which lies nevertheless this side of perfection. The typical attitude here is cold and calculating purposiveness. The advocates of contingent means are most often practical statesmen and political leaders whose eyes are focused on immediate tasks. They may be decent and 'moderate' in every sense of the word, or they may be thoroughly immoral. However, this kind of immorality, with its occasional hardness and cynicism, still differs from the intense and idealistic immorality of extremism. The latter tends to be characterized by a kind of blind consistency which is far removed from the world of practical statesmanship and political give-and-take.

To appreciate this difference, however, we have now to take note of yet another category of means encountered in political action. We can call these *exceptional* or *critical* means. They differ from contingent means in that while the latter stand to their ends in a relationship of logical independence, the former logically contradict their ends. This means also that exceptional means are contrary to integral means. Now what are exceptional means, in concrete terms? Broadly speaking, we can say that, inasmuch as all political ends are particular definitions of the 'good society', acknowledging the validity of certain generally accepted basic moral notions, exceptional means are those that even their advocates admit are incompatible with these moral notions. Peace, contentment, security and the orderly settlement of human relationships are the aims of political effort. Violence, terror, torture, cruelty and assassination are the methods which are the most obviously 'exceptional' to these aims.

Revolutionary (or counter-revolutionary) transformations, in a broad sense, provide most frequently the context in which exceptional means are resorted to or called for. It is these days fairly common to hear adherents of the most far-fetched revolutionary political ends, future states of society depicted in the most extravagantly glowing terms of love, happiness and tranquillity, demand the employment of physical violence and a reign of terror as political means. Evidently, the extent to which the consciousness of the *hindrances* to the realization of the end overshadows in the choice of means the consciousness of the end itself will be the most apparent in the case of exceptional means. Proponents of exceptional means themselves assert the incompatibility of the means with the end, once the end is brought into being. Once there is a society of perfect love, you don't go on bumping off wicked politicians, partly because wicked politicians will not be there any more, and partly because you yourself will have become incapable of committing such deeds. Once the people are really free, it will be not merely empirically unnecessary but morally impossible to cling on to a reign of terror, though you might think that a reign of terror is essential to the initial task of liberation.

Now again it would be a mistake to regard all those who employ exceptional means in the pursuit of their political ends as 'extremists'. The single and occasional recourse to such means is quite compatible with a position of overall moderation.[1] (For moderates with limited ends who occasionally find themselves compelled to use violence, etc., as a political means, these means, of course, will be 'contingent', and not 'exceptional'. It all depends on the nature of the end.) Undoubtedly, however, the *consistent* and continuous advocacy of exceptional means marks the beginning of extremism. A philosophy of exceptional means is always the most natural and plausible justification of extremist policies and attitudes.

The question now is: why should people engaged in politics ever come to embrace a philosophy of exceptional means? We have said that with exceptional means the emphasis is on hindrances to ends, rather than on ends themselves. This means that we have now to return to a consideration of the nature of political ends, concentrating on the relationship between ends and existing societies, or what was above called the 'uncharted dimension' of political ends.

The nature of political ends is not exhausted by their divergent and numerous empirical characteristics, such as the ending of class divisions in one case or the breeding of pure racial types in another. Far more important and relevant to our present concerns is another set of characteristics they all possess. These characteristics together constitute what we could call the *moral* dimension of political ends: 'moral' because it is

[1] cf. 'The point is that under certain circumstances violence – acting without argument or speech and without counting the consequences – is the only way to set the scales of justice right again.' Hannah Arendt, *On Violence* (London, 1970), p. 64.

these characteristics of ends that determine a political activist's moral attitude to the society in which his activity takes place. It is the moral dimension of a political end that provides the answer to this one basic and decisive question: does a political activist look upon his desired end as the sole and total remedy of all the ills and defects at present disfiguring his society, or does he regard it as a partial remedy designed to deal with specific ills? The moral dimension, in other words, measures the supposed potency, effectiveness, and hence urgency and importance of political ends.

It is true, of course, that everyone engaged actively in politics must be committed to ends appearing to him potent and important as cures for the imperfections of society. But not everyone expects his end to miraculously change all imperfection into perfection. Those political activists who thus think in terms of totalities – wars to end all wars – and endow their political ends with the attributes of panacea, are called utopians. Utopianism is used here in the double sense, denoting those who believe both that perfection (perfect peace, perfect happiness) is a practical possibility, and that one particular political medicine (the classless society, world government, decolonization) will achieve it. Utopians in politics are like people who think that slimming diets will make them into athletes, tycoons and the successful seducers of women, all at once. The other group of political activists contains people with a fundamentally different outlook: those who see their political ends as partial, circumscribed, imperfect remedies, cures that cure particular illnesses but are no guarantee against death. (Slimming diets may be good for slimming, but nothing else.) This is the position of realism.

Now it is the central argument of this essay that utopianism in politics is the logical antecedent of extremism, moderation being the consequence of realism. This should not be taken in a very strict sense. As in any other walk of practical life, in politics also it is possible to hold on to self-contradictory positions. The point here concerns merely the internal consistency of typical attitudes encountered in political life, and as will be shown below, the logical typology here presented has some plausibility behind it.

One essential point, however, has to be grasped here and now: the empirical and moral dimensions of political ends stand in an opposed relationship to the way a person engaged in politics perceives the society surrounding him at the present. The empirical characteristics of ends are evidently derived from one's knowledge and experience of one's society, sometimes appearing, of course, in an inverted form. Ideas of heaven are fashioned on ideas of earth. But *the* idea of a heaven, that is, the idea of an alternative to the present, and the qualities that determine one's moral attitude to this heaven, such as its certainty, totality and degree of perfection, are not derived from a knowledge of the earth. This is suggested by the evidence of history. Conceptions of the good society vary enormously over the centuries, but utopianism and realism as basic attitudes are there to be found in every historical epoch. The moral dimension of political ends, therefore, has to be seen as something given in each case, as the starting-point for political commitment. (There may or may not be ultimate explanations in psychoanalytic, religious or any other terms.) And this means, of course, that when it comes to the moral evaluation of the present, its adulation or condemnation as the case may be, this evaluation will derive from and be dependent upon one's conception of the moral dimension of one's end. Once this is seen, the distinction between moderation and extremism falls into place.

The logical attraction pulling utopians towards extremism and realists towards moderation can now be described in a few brief sentences. Let us first see the utopian position. A total vision paints the future pure, dazzling white. The present: existing society, will hence appear to the utopian as pitch black. The belief in a perfect remedy – in a cure that is certain, imminent and all-embracing – will render one's criticism of existing society correspondingly total, relentless, uncompromising. In more concrete and moral terms: to the extent that the future appears wholly good, the present will appear wholly bad, depraved, sinful. In terms of this vision, then, present society shows itself incapable of being saved by its own efforts, by anything contained within itself. Its total corruption means that the decay has reached further than its political and social institutions, right down to its moral notions, its very ideas of right and wrong. Its ideas of moral propriety, in fact, have the function of covering up for its deep-lying depravity, revealing (to the utopian) at the same time society's most vulnerable points.

If you consider society totally depraved, you will have no compunctions about what *this* society regards as immoral and criminal. On the contrary, since your purpose is to eliminate present arrangements in the shortest time possible, it will be natural for you to choose means which are most appropriate for speedy demolition work. The greater the moral shock it causes to defenders of the establishment, the more reliable will seem any course of action that promises to sweep the whole structure away. Fraud, murder, terrorism and the like are methods which acquire moral legitimacy as well as empirical appropriateness as political means in the ratio that existing society is denied any genuinely moral attributes. Even the most outrageous methods are 'worth' it, literally, if you believe that what you are fighting for is heaven and what you are up against are the forces of hell.[1]

[1] cf. the striking Introduction to Conor Cruise O'Brien and W. D. Vanech (eds.), *Power and Consciousness*. London, 1969.

Realism does not paint the future white. The political ends informed by this attitude will appear merely a lighter shade of grey than the present societies which are contrasted with them. The realist's criticism of existing society is, in the best sense of the term, quantitative, as opposed to the qualitative criticism entailed by the utopian position. Realism here, of course, must be distinguished from the cynicism and conservatism often associated with the term 'Realpolitik'. Two shades of grey may be very different from each other, a quantitative distance between present and future may be a very significant distance indeed. However, the realist's choice of means will be governed and limited by the moral nature of his vision of the future. He must be like Weber's politician who lets 'realities work upon him with inner concentration and calmness.'[1]

Though the realist may in many cases be resolutely opposed to all the institutions, ideologies and practices of existing society, his attitude to the present will not be wholly negative. As he sees imperfection surviving even in a brighter future, he will notice rays of light in the darker present.[2] His methods will be characterized by caution and a special regard for those features of existing society that still appear valid. In particular, he will see the existence of basic moral notions in this society (even if they are paid only lip-service to) as proof that the society is not beyond repair. The aspirations of this society, as opposed to its practice, will be conceived by him as its bridges to the future. It would then make no sense to want to burn the bridges: on the contrary, it is through them that the realist will endeavour to do his political work. In practice this will then mean demands for *more* and for *less*: for more freedom, more equality, more democracy, and for less bureaucracy, less arbitrariness, etc. – to be realized either in or outside the framework of existing institutions, but always *inside* the fabric of existing moral aspirations.

The extremist wants to realize his utopia immediately; the moderate

[1] Weber, op. cit., p. 115., cf. the attitude of reforming socialism, as presented by Peter Gay, which 'goes beyond ascertained fact, making an imaginative leap into the future, but it is careful to curb its imagination'. Peter Gay, *The Dilemma of Democratic Socialism* (New York, 1952), p. 154.

[2] As Eduard Bernstein, a moderate socialist, argued at the time, liberal institutions are 'flexible and capable of change and development. They do not need to be destroyed, but only to be further developed.' Eduard Bernstein, *Evolutionary Socialism*, Introduction by Sidney Hook (New York, 1961), p. 163. Or take an opinion from the recent past: 'Of course, this new socialism requires the full preservation of civic liberties and a plurality of political parties; all the living heritage of liberal democracy.' Perry Anderson, 'Problems of Socialist Strategy', in Perry Anderson and Robin Blackburn (eds.), *Towards Socialism* (London, 1965), p. 246.

THE DISTINCTION BETWEEN MODERATION AND EXTREMISM

has no utopia but immediate aims to realize.[1] Realism also ensures that the occasional recourse to methods that can justly be called 'extreme' will be taken up only in 'extreme' situations where absolutely no other methods are available, and not hardened into a permanent habit or style. Only utopians can consistently refer to whole existing societies in terms borrowed from a quasi-military vocabulary, talking about permanent crises, states of emergency and imminent disasters. This kind of thinking, with its built-in justification of extremism, would be illogical from the realist point of view.

We can go further here and remark on the very apparent incongruity and logical inconsistency that would characterize an interchange of positions, with utopianism embracing moderation and realism combining with the consistent advocacy of extreme methods. Both these combinations must at one point contradict – not their respective political ends, but the existing societies which are morally defined in terms of these ends. Utopianism thinks in terms of black-and-white. But moderation must presuppose greyness all round. Realism sees existing society as containing both valid and invalid elements, as being both forward-looking and anachronistic. But extremism is justified only if we do not allow for any potentiality of existing society to change for the better through its own efforts. Thus the utopian who advocates the employment of moderate methods will tend to be the incorrigible dreamer, the religious reformer who has confounded the world of politics with another, supermundane world. He may propose to change society by 'love', forgetting that his vision already pronounced society blacker than hell, a place where not even a modicum of genuine love can be found.

On the other hand, the realist who advocates the continuous use of extreme methods is either a fool or a criminal. He is a fool if he is blind to the fact that extremism in political action negates his own understanding of present society: it would mean cracking eggs by putting them into nuclear incinerators. The omelette would not be very nourishing. And he is a criminal if his apparent realism is merely a cover for the aggrandizement of personal power. Clandestine extremism can take at least temporary advantage of a political situation where realistic thinking is taken for granted by the participants. (This kind of extremism, however, is less frequent than people would think.) It would, at any rate, be strange if somebody seriously called for the assassination of a Conservative Prime Minister in order to ensure Labour victory at the next General Election. Equally odd would it be, however, for someone who wanted

[1] cf. Bernstein: 'I am not concerned with what will happen in the more distant future, but with what can and ought to happen in the present, for the present and the nearest future.' op. cit., p. 163.

to overthrow the whole establishment to confine his activities to the lobbying of his parliamentary representative.

Finally, we should attempt briefly to draw the distinction between moral absolutism on the one hand and the moderate criticism of extremist philosophies on the other. These two, at any rate, are genuine criticisms of the *extremism* contained in some political ideologies, as opposed to objections raised against the substance of the same. Substantive disagreement over ends is no indication as to the extremism or moderation of the protagonists. De Maistre's critique of the French Revolution is a case in point. Technical disagreement over means is not an indication either: Stalin and Trotzky were both extremists, Kautsky and Bernstein both moderates. The relevant kind of criticism here is moral criticism of the moral aspects of political ends.

Moral absolutism and moderation share the fundamental conviction that all political ends must be limited in some way. In the case of moral absolutism, this is held in the form of a belief in universally and eternally valid categorical imperatives. In the field of political action, this belief is expressed as the unconditional and total condemnation of certain methods, most often those involving the use of physical force, and it signifies the holder's refusal to have recourse to such methods, whatever the needs and whatever the circumstances. The moral absolutist regards ethical commands like 'do not kill' or 'do not tell lies' as imperatives which cannot tolerate even single exceptions.

Now moral absolutism is without doubt an honourable position to hold, except that it prevents its holder from consistently participating in politics, either as an activist with a definite political commitment, or as a subject or citizen who is affected by the political action of others. The moral absolutist, in the first place, may be an activist pursuing a certain political end, say, the 'classless society'. He may be firmly convinced that this end does provide at least some of the answers to our present problems, and he may also be convinced, having rationally considered all possibilities, that at this particular place and this particular historical juncture the only way to achieve this end is through violent revolution. But he is opposed to 'violence' of all kinds. What can he do? He is reduced to a state of political impotence, and can easily end up in total disillusionment or apathy or something even worse.

But then, secondly, moral absolutism is no better guide to action for those who are at the receiving end of tyrannical or extremist policies. Moral absolutism forbids the use of extreme methods even in genuine emergency situations, even as exceptional means to prevent or defeat extremism. The person holding beliefs of this nature cannot forcibly deal with the violent, cannot use weapons to rise against a reign of terror, cannot cheat the liars, cannot contemplate assassinating the would-be assassin. The refusal to go to the length of using extreme methods even in instances where they would be warranted means affording a seemingly equal comfort to extremists and their opponents. As, however, extremism is by definition always more effective than its opponent (since the extremist will use *any* method), this attitude really amounts to an unwitting bias in favour of extremism. Moral absolutism, therefore, will lead to opting out of politics altogether and occupying a sealed, out-of-reach ivory tower. The only meaningful alternative is to accept an opening towards the position of moderation,

The moderate, just as the moral absolutist, may be committed to all sorts of political ends, ranging from those involving the total transformation of society to those which envisage a constant series of minor adjustments. Or he may be a defender of the *status quo*. His particular distinction, or gift, is the recognition that though historical changes may always achieve something definite, some real improvement in a way of life or the organization of society, they do not – never have done and never will – achieve *the* great change that extremists and utopians of all kinds dream about. 'The new becomes itself old, often before it is consciously recognized as new; and history shows us no example of the sudden substitution of utopian and revolutionary romance.'[1] It is this knowledge, based on the weightiest kind of historical, philosophical and experiential evidence, that will advise him against extremism even in the pursuit of revolutionary political ends.

Since no single political end can be a total remedy obliterating the scars on human nature and society, it follows that even genuine advances have a price which survivors and future generations have to pay. The price cannot be avoided, but it may be minimized, and the way to do this is by persistently calling attention to the limitations of political ends, the dark shadows surrounding bright stars. As opposed to moral absolutism which correctly sees that political ends cannot be supreme, but which errs by subordinating them to static and paralysing categorical imperatives, moderation sees the limits of political ends in the shape of their own opposites, in what the various political ends leave out of their visionary formulations. Now while extremist courses of action may always succeed in realizing a goal (it *is* possible to build socialism on bayonets), they will do irreparable damage to areas of life or aspects of human nature which are obscured by the goal itself. A moderate thus, in a context of revolutionary socialism, will want to call attention to

[1] Sidney Webb, 'The Historic Basis of Socialism', in G. B. Shaw *et al.*, *Fabian Essays,* with a New Introduction by Asa Briggs (London, 1962), p. 63. cf. 'A non-violent, perfect society is not a possibility, but freer and more equitable societies are.' Milovan Djilas, *The Unperfect Society* (London, 1969), p. 185. Djilas's work, though overshadowed in importance by his other publications, is an eloquent plea for moderation.

individual conscience and excellence; to co-operation and welfare in a context of liberalism; to equality and participation in a context of conservatism. But moderation is and will always remain a thankless task, and while moderates may often achieve success, laurels will accrue to them but rarely.

Liberalism and Morality

BHIKHU PAREKH

By Liberalism I mean a body of beliefs that makes its appearance in the sixteenth and seventeenth century and centres essentially around the bourgeois-individualistic conception of man. Liberalism takes the natural physical individual as the ultimate social reality and views him as an essentially possessive and private being shut up in his own subjectivity. The limits of his body are considered the limits of his self. The outer surface of his skin marks out the area that is ineliminably his own, and what goes on within it is regarded as entirely his own business. As he 'owns' his body he has proprietary rights over its constituents and, since his life is 'his' and nobody else's, he believes he can do what he likes with it. His mind is also 'his', and therefore the ideas it generates and the feelings it feels are claimed as his own. He owns his senses and so therefore the sensations and the experience that they gather in the outside world. As a self-enclosed and socially insulated creature he is seen as an inescapably private being who faces the world in his sovereign loneliness.

As each individual is considered a sovereign who knows or ought to know his interest best, and as almost a fetish, a cult, is made of the ability to 'stand on one's own feet', an individual is believed to have no obligations that he has not explicitly or implicitly accepted. As such sovereign atoms can be related to each other only externally, all their obligations and duties are deemed to result solely from their own acts of will. All obligations are therefore conceived in terms of the generic notion of contract, of which consent – explicit or tacit – covenant, agreement, promise, convention and consensus are different forms. Indeed in the Liberal view relations between sovereign individuals are substantially like those between sovereign states; and like the latter, they involve skilful handling, acute diplomacy, and sensitive regard for protocol.[1]

[1] It is not generally realized that a Liberal's theory of international relations is generally only his theory of interpersonal relations projected on the international

The state is simply an instrument to ensure that contracts are enforced and each individual secured in his clearly demarcated private space. Like all institutions it is judged by its ability to serve the interests of sovereign and egoistic beings.

The Liberal moral life centres essentially around the notion of reciprocity. You invite me home for dinner, and I have an obligation to reciprocate. My behaviour would be disapproved of if I did not invite you, and it would appear somewhat odd if you invited me a second time without my having 'returned' your first invitation. Or, again, if you visited me in a hospital, I should 'return' your visit; or if you sent me a card, I would be failing in my obligation if I did not. In general everything that one person does for another is considered a 'favour', and is charged to his account. He remains 'in debt', 'indebted', until he 'returns' it. He feels weighed down by obligations and favours, and looks for opportunities to return and reciprocate so that he can then face the world as a person who owes 'nothing to any body', whose moral sovereignty and independence have remained uncompromised. The Liberal feels inferior when he is 'under' an obligation, and awaits an opportunity when he can be 'free' again to look his benefactor straight in his eye as an equal. Moral life for him is not an organic whole but an aggregate of specific and identifiable atomic obligations, each of which he generally remembers very clearly and seeks to discharge at the first available opportunity. Ideally, he wishes to live a life in which he has discharged all obligations charged by others to his account, and his moral balance-sheet is clear.

The debts that are too profound to be repaid, the debts, for example, to parents and to community, make him extremely nervous and uneasy as he cannot settle or 'repay' them in quite the way he settles his contractual debts with his grocer. His tendency is either to ignore them, or to trivialize them by trying to fit them into a dubious contractualist mould. Thus, for example, the question of obligations to community is reduced to that of obeying its laws, and the problem of political obligation is formulated as why one should obey the law. The Liberal believes he has 'repaid' his 'debt' to his community if he has obeyed its laws; it rarely occurs to him to ask if being a good member of a polity does not also involve trying to improve it by taking an intelligent and affectionate interest in the conduct of its affairs, or by giving thought as to how its inevitable injustices can be removed, or how the lives of its members can

---

scene. One has only to compare, for example, J. S. Mill's *On Liberty* and 'A Few Words on Non-intervention' to notice substantial similarities of approach and conclusion.

be bettered, or how the authorities can be dissuaded from pursuing mad policies.

It will have been seen that I am using the term Liberal to refer not to a political party or a programme but to a *Weltanschauung*, a way of life and an attitude of mind, a way of understanding man and his world, that appeared in Europe at a certain time. As with any body of beliefs, many of its basic values long preceded its birth. Thus the concern with critical rationality, individual choice, freedom, tolerance, love of comforts goes back to Socrates and beyond. What distinguishes Liberalism and makes it a unique 'historical individual' is not its belief in these values but the way it redefines and rearranges them within the bourgeois individualistic conception of man. Liberalism, that is to say, is only one of many possible ways of defining liberal values, and it is possible to hold liberal values – that is, to be a liberal with a small 'l' – and yet to interpret and justify them differently from the way Liberalism does. Thus, for example, one may define freedom positively with Aristotle rather than negatively with Bentham, or justify it with Aquinas as the opportunities of a social being rather than with Locke as a natural right of a sovereign individual.

A non-Liberal therefore is not necessarily illiberal, and a person who attacks Liberalism is not necessarily an enemy of liberty. Indeed, it is perfectly intelligible for a person not to be a Liberal precisely because he is a liberal; that is to say, it is precisely because he believes that the modern Liberal society cannot safeguard the traditional liberal values which he cherishes that he might want to overthrow it. A socialist for example rejects Liberalism as a way of looking at man and yet he is generally a liberal. In short, it is perfectly rational for a liberal not to be a Liberal[1] and for a Liberal to turn out not to be a liberal in a particular historical context.

The moral life as it has developed in the Liberal society (and as it has been understood by Liberal philosophers) has inevitably acquired a number of distinctive features. I wish to single out two of them, namely, the amazing contraction of the scope of morality and its positivism, for detailed and critical examination in the next two sections.

I

As we observed earlier, the Liberal takes the body as his fundamental point of reference. It is this physicalism that determines his attitude to a

[1] It is thus possible for a communist society to be liberalized (in the sense for example, of allowing greater freedom of public criticism and more than one political party) without being Liberalized (in the sense, for example, of allowing private ownership of means of production).

number of issues. Violence is defined in physical terms so that the infliction of physical harm is violence, but of psychic or moral harm is not. Or, again, a man's freedom is deemed to be restricted when he is physically restrained from moving as he pleases, but not when his ideas or beliefs or emotions are conditioned and moulded. Morally, it is physical more than any other type of suffering that dominates the Liberal moral imagination. If he saw someone crying, dying, starving, he might feel he ought to do something about it, but if he saw a child frustrated from developing his abilities for want of money, or a man in despair for lack of gainful employment, he would not generally see that a moral problem is involved and that he ought to do something about it.

Further, even at the level of suffering, morality, like almost everything else, is conceived as essentially negative in character. Understanding the individual as a sovereign creature who must enjoy unhindered freedom in a clearly marked out space, the Liberal society has concentrated on setting up protective barriers between individuals. This attitude of separating individuals and excluding them from each other's domain has meant that the dominant ethos in society is basically negative; the state is not to interfere with individual life; it is not to regulate economic life; individuals are not to meddle with each other, etc. Morally, too, the emphasis has been on negative rather than on positive injunctions, on not causing suffering rather than on positively helping others.

Even when morality is understood as not causing physical suffering, a further limit is imposed on its practice. The Liberal society regards man as an essentially self-centred creature who cannot but pursue his own interest. Since the pursuit of self-interest is regarded as natural and inevitable, it and the entire realm of economic relationship that it generates are placed outside the scope of moral evaluation. While the medieval society thought of economic life in terms of *pure* and *impure* wealth, *proper* and *improper* ways of acquiring it, *fair* and *unfair* prices, and *just* and *unjust* wages, and continued to attack possessiveness even when it did not attack possessions, the Liberal society rests on the belief that economic relationships are 'natural', and like any other process of nature, not therefore amenable to moral scrutiny. Prices are determined solely by the considerations of demand and supply; the decision whether or not to retrench employees is regarded as purely commercial and not raising any moral issues at all; paying the lowest wages is not wrong if one can get away with it; creating degrading working conditions is not wrong if required by calculations of profit; a landlord can let his property run down or charge exorbitant rent without any moral regard to the needs of his tenants; a landowner sees no moral issues involved in letting his land lie useless rather than giving it for parks or schools or other public uses.

It is indeed remarkable how the Liberal society has taken area after area of social life out of the jurisdiction of morality. We have already remarked on economic life. Politics, too, is seen as a process of taking decisions on the basis of pressures exerted by the contending parties, and each side, determined to negotiate from a position of strength, feels encouraged to use whatever levers of pressure are available to it, including the use or threat of violence. The same ethos prevails at the level of international relations. The government is committed to the pursuit of national interest, and whatever is required by the national interest, as defined by the political community in question, is deemed justified. Just as individual interest is placed outside morality, so is national interest, and moral principles are not allowed to enter into its definition or manner of pursuit. It is not asked if a nation has obligations to those outside it, or if it is right to consider its own interests as having greater moral claim than those of others, or if it should pursue its interest in a way that causes them grave and irreparable harm.

It is not only the area of human conduct subject to moral considerations that has shrunk; the range of humans whose well-being moral conduct is supposed to seek has shrunk too. For a variety of reasons too complex to discuss here, the ideas of time and space have shrunk in the Liberal society, and the application of moral principles has come to be confined, in time, largely to those alive, and in space, largely to the members of one's own society. As the past is deemed 'dead', it is denied any moral status and therefore the notion of obligations to ancestors is considered to make no sense. The future is hypothetical, non-existent, and therefore is considered morally important only as the future of those alive, and not as signifying countless generations yet unborn. Thus the three-dimensionality of time has collapsed into the present, and morally only the claims – present or future – of those alive are taken into account.

The idea of space has undergone a more or less similar metamorphosis. The entire mass of humanity is replaced by men living within the framework of a specific territory, and their claims are treated as the only ones that matter, or as having a degree of moral urgency denied to those of others. While poverty, misery and attacks on freedom in one's own community are given moral attention, their prevalence in other communities is not seen to raise or require any moral response. It is no doubt true that we do in practice take some account of the interests of future generations and of men in other lands, but this is more symbolic than real. It is largely the result of the influence of non-Liberal, mainly Christian, moralities that have still retained some appeal, and their full force is rarely allowed to seep into our moral consciousness and conduct.

We have outlined the way the Liberal understands moral life and the various ways in which he restricts its scope. Strictly speaking, none of these restrictions is justified and the Liberal lands himself in a number of paradoxes. The Liberal maintains that an individual has no obligations that he has not explicitly or implicitly undertaken. Yet he admits that he should try to help a person in distress, or help an old lady cross a road, or phone the police when a man is being attacked, or intervene when one child is being beaten up by another. Now it is not clear how the Liberal can justify these obligations and why he would not extend the grounds on which they are based to generate further obligations. None of these is an obligation I have consciously entered into, or incumbent on me as an occupant of a role or office. To be sure, some Liberal philosophers do not even discuss such obligations, and imply that morality is entirely a matter of keeping promises and agreements. But this is a consistency bought at a high moral price. Most Liberals would admit that moral conduct does extend to helping people in need. But once this is admitted, it implies, however minimally, that I am 'my brother's keeper' – the view that the Liberal denies – and it gives rise, as we shall see later, to a large range of other obligations that the Liberal cannot consistently ignore.

Again, if causing physical harm to a person is bad, so is causing him serious psychic, moral or spiritual damage, and there is no reason why only physical harm should be singled out for moral purposes. What is more, physical harm is bad because, among other things, it causes pain to the victim, restricts his freedom, and hinders him from realizing his objectives. But then, causing him psychic damage by, for example, exploiting him, manipulating him, or denying him opportunities for growth does precisely the same, and therefore the same considerations that make physical harm bad also make psychological and moral harm bad. For linguistic clarity we might give them different names and call one violence and the other something else, but morally they are both equally evil.

The dubious view that as long as an individual does not directly cause suffering to another he is being moral also breaks down. I can cause suffering to another directly and by my own actions, or indirectly by taking part in a common enterprise. Now clearly there is a significant difference between the two situations. In one case I am uniquely and personally responsible for my action; in the other I share responsibility with others. But to suggest that in the second case I am not responsible *at all* is clearly a mistake, since I have been a willing party to the enterprise and have enjoyed its benefits. I remain responsible for it unless I have dissociated myself from it by protesting against its general direction, or by urging others to run it differently, or by opting out of it. To see a co-operative venture as absolving each of the participants from the responsibility for its consequences is as much a fallacy as to transfer the responsibility for collective actions on to each individual's conscience.

It is, of course, true that the impersonal forces of the market impose considerable restraints on the individual and often force him to do things he personally disapproves of. But the real question is how we are to respond to this situation. We can either let it continue, in which case we are morally responsible for the suffering these forces create; or we can direct our energies towards bringing them under conscious moral control, in which case we have abandoned some of the basic tenets of Liberal morality.

There is a further problem created by placing economic activity outside morality. Since man is regarded as essentially an economic being, this means that the very centre of his being is regarded as amoral. It also means that a paradox is planted in the very heart of the Liberal moral theory. As a moral being, the individual is required not to cause suffering to others. And yet the very activity that is the centre of his attention is responsible for much of the suffering in the first instance.

The Liberal can respond to this situation in one of three ways. He accepts the suffering – the poverty, the misery, the injustice – as natural and does nothing about it, in which case he jettisons his status as a moral agent. Or, secondly, he tries to alleviate the suffering by personal charity and organized humanitarian action in which case his morality is paradoxical, causing suffering and then alleviating it. Indeed, as his morality is no more than a nurse-maid healing the wounds inflicted by the hands it is unwilling to stay and is even willing to assist, it is profoundly immoral. Or, thirdly, he sees the patent self-contradiction of his behaviour and tries to regulate economic life morally by using the state to insist, for example, on healthy conditions of work or on certain minimum wages, in which case he surrenders one of the basic premises of his moral and political theory, and turns to a non-Liberal morality to resolve the contradictions of his own morality.

The basic problem, however, is why economic activity (or politics) should be placed outside morality in the first instance. An individual is a moral being, and to be moral is to be concerned as to how one's actions affect others. Unless we take the view that in economic life individuals appear not as men but as things, economic actions do raise moral issues. But then to take that view would mean that the very activity that the Liberal regards as distinctly human is essentially non-human, dehumanizing! Further, as we shall discuss fully later, it is a mistake to define interest first and then argue that one has no obligations that do not accord with it. In discussing economic activity we are not discussing the activities of some strange amoral creatures but of men who, among other things, are also moral beings. And for a moral being, moral considerations enter into the very definition of his interest, and nothing can be accepted as an interest that is not morally approvable. If a man said that it was in his interest to enslave or slaughter the whole world or a whole class of men we would think that he was morally deficient. We recognize the individual's pursuit of his interest as legitimate not because he has some natural right to it but because we believe that this is the best way to achieve his own and society's good. This means that pursuit of self-interest is not a pre-moral principle enjoying absolute superiority over all others, but needs to be legitimized by being placed within a moral framework.[1]

We saw earlier how the practice of morality in modern society is severely restricted in time and space. This restriction too is arbitrary and ultimately unjustified. If I knew that by running my family affairs in a certain way my children and grandchildren would suffer, surely I would have a duty to run them differently. If we knew that by using up our national resources we were likely to impoverish succeeding generations, or if we knew that by trying to produce cheaply and quickly we were likely to pollute our environment beyond repair, or impair the health and well-being of succeeding generations, we would have a moral duty to sacrifice our immediate advantage. The simple point of these examples is that duties to men are not affected by time, and that one generation holds the resources of the community in trust for its successors.

It is, of course, true that moral actions, like all other types of action, are limited both by the knowledge of the likely consequences of one's actions and by one's other obligations. Thus I have a duty to help a man in distress, but if I knew that he was a murderer, my prima facie duty would be overridden; or if I was in a hurry because my wife was having a major operation, I would be right to conclude that my obligation to her was more stringent and morally more weighty. Similarly, my duties to men yet unborn are limited both by my relative ignorance of what technology and life in general will be like then, and by the more stringent obligations I owe to my contemporaries. However, the ignorance is never complete and one is able to make fair guesses about the conditions of life in the next generation. And in any case, the argument from ignorance works both ways and therefore remains inconclusive. Although the claims of succeeding generations may be overridden by the more stringent claims of my contemporaries, they therefore continue to remain a factor to be taken into account in every moral decision affecting them.

If time cannot detract from moral duties, nor can space. A suffering man in China or Peru or Algeria has a claim on my attention just as much as the man next door. Suffering is suffering, whether it is in England or Algeria, and human suffering is human suffering, whether

---

[1] For a discussion of what happens when politics is de-moralized, see my 'Fanon's Theory of Violence' in Bhikhu Parekh, ed. *Dissent and Disorder* (World University Service of Canada, 1971), p. 37 ff.

the man concerned is Chinese or English or Algerian. No doubt, this general duty to alleviate suffering is subject to the same general limits as the duty to succeeding generations. I have a special obligation to the members of my own community because I have entered into a special relationship with them. I have a greater knowledge of their habits and patterns of life, and being members of the same political community, they expect help from me and are acutely frustrated when their expectations are not met. Conversely, I have no special relationship with a Chinese or an Algerian and have no special obligations to him. Besides, my knowledge of his need is extremely limited. I am not always sure what type of help he needs, or whether my help will reach him, or whether it would not be counter-productive, or whether it would make a difference to his life for the better.

However, these and other empirical limits can easily be exaggerated. There are cases where I have a reliable knowledge of the type of help he needs. No great imagination is needed to know that a starving man needs food, and a naked man needs clothes. And in any case, a moral duty cannot be abdicated under the cover of ignorance, but requires me to try to obtain more knowledge about the condition of life of those known to be suffering. As for the argument based on expectation, it is circular, since it amounts to saying that I should not help a man in need because he does not expect me to, and he does not expect me to because I have never helped in the past! The way to break the vicious circle is to start helping and creating expectations in him, and thereby incurring the obligation to help him.

Poverty in the undeveloped communities then is not and cannot be merely their problem, but a universal problem that has a claim on the moral attention and resources of all moral beings everywhere. And similarly their struggle for freedom and justice has a claim on the support of all those who cherish these values. If I hold that liberty or life is a value, I am required by the very logic of morality to uphold your claim to liberty or life; and this means, negatively that I should do nothing, unless required by other more stringent claims, to hinder you from achieving these values, and positively that I should support and help you whenever I can consistently with my other obligations. It is morally inconsistent to say that liberty is a value for an Englishman but not for an Indian, or that I have an obligation to fight for my liberty but that your struggle for liberty is of no moral concern to me.

It might be argued that although the point just made is pertinent, it is too abstract to be relevant to our ordinary moral life, in which we are rarely faced with moral decisions affecting the lives of people outside our own community. But this is not true. I can influence, however marginally, the life of an unemployed Indian by deciding to buy a little more expensive Indian shirt rather than a cheaper Japanese or American shirt, or the life of a black African in South Africa by deciding not to buy South African goods. Or, again, I can decide to contribute a part of my salary to Oxfam, or I can decide to go, or to encourage my son or students to go to a country where my or their skill and experience could be useful. That these and other acts are of little consequence unless undertaken by a large number of men is true. But the answer to that is not to stop acting oneself, but to persuade others to undertake them as well. Others' ignorance of their duties cannot absolve a moral agent from doing his.

However, although such acts at a purely personal level do make an impact, the most effective medium of action is obviously the government. It is open to morally conscious individuals to persuade and press their government to give greater technical and financial aid to poor countries, or to give them better trading terms, or to stop bolstering up despotic and tyrannical regimes, or to pursue policies designed to encourage free and just societies elsewhere. The state is a medium through which one group of men interacts with another, and unless it was argued that men miraculously become demoralized in politics or that people in other communities are not men but things, they remain and therefore retain their obligation to act as moral beings in politics as anywhere else. The uncertainty and chaos of international life does make the practice of morality difficult; but again, the answer to that is not to idealize the situation as the Nietzschean philosophers of power-struggle do, or to rationalize it into the view that morality is irrelevant to international relations, but rather to regret it and to explore realistic ways of bringing international life under moral control.

The question then is not whether universal morality is practicable, since in a world so obviously interdependent it clearly is. Nor is it a question whether it is desirable, since it clearly is vital for the very survival of the species. Indeed, universality, as Hare and Mrs. Foot have shown, is inherent in the very description of a value or a principle as moral, so that any moral theory that defines good in terms of the good of a particular community is void *ab initio*; national egoism is just as self-contradictory as individual egoism. The point rather is that to a society geared to a constantly rising level of consumption and to measuring its progress by the one-dimensional standard of constantly increasing gross national product, it appears an unacceptable sacrifice to pay higher taxes in order that the poor elsewhere can be helped, or to pay higher prices in order that unemployment elsewhere can be avoided, or to accept lower profit in order that healthy environment can be preserved for future generations or in order that basic industries can be allowed to grow in poorer communities.

LIBERALISM AND MORALITY

Morally speaking the position is clear. A community that would not accept a slight fall in its standard of living or in its profits, when it can be shown that by so doing it would be helping poorer communities to secure justice for their people, is like a man who is so absorbed in his toothache, or, worse, in his little amusement, that he would not lend a helping hand to a person in distress. And neither is moral in any sense of the term. The Liberal, here as elsewhere, arbitrarily restricts the application of his moral principles when they begin to require him to compromise his interests.

II

Apart from the extreme contraction of its scope, the further characteristic of the Liberal morality is what can best be called its positivism. This is not a particularly good term, but it is far more suggestive than any other. We saw earlier that morality is defined by the Liberal in terms of interests, in that being moral is taken to mean, at any rate, to involve impartial consideration of others' interests. Interests, in turn, are generally defined as conditions necessary to satisfy wants. Thus morality is ultimately anchored in a quasi-natural principle that is itself placed outside morality. Some of the difficulties of this naturalistic positivism are clearly reflected in R. M. Hare's moral theory.[1]

Drawing a rather neat distinction between interests and ideals, in a way reminiscent of Kant's distinction between perfection and happiness, Hare argues that ideals are essentially personal and ought not to influence one's relations with others. In one's relationship with them, one is to do no more than pursue their interests 'To have an interest is, crudely speaking, for there to be something which one wants, or is likely in the future to want, or which is (or is likely to be) a means necessary or sufficient for the attainment of something which one wants (or is likely to want)'.[2] Being moral to others thus means satisfying their wants; crudely, it means giving them what they want. Ideals for Hare are basically aesthetic in nature and to act on them in one's relationship with others is to impose one's dream or vision on them, and that is the road to fanaticism. Indeed he takes the view that it was the pursuit of ideals that was responsible for the Second World War. Hare uses this distinction between ideals and interests as a basis for his far more important political distinction between a moderate and a fanatic, a moderate being one who is mindful of others' interests and a fanatic being a man concerned only with the realization of his own ideals.

Now there are a number of grounds on which Hare's analysis could be

[1] *Freedom and Reason* (Oxford, 1963). Chapters 8 and 9.
[2] ibid., p. 122.

faulted. One could show that ideals are not necessarily aesthetic in nature and that the logic of an argument based on ideals is significantly different from the logic of an aesthetic argument. One can, for example, go about realizing one's ideals in a way that takes account of others' limitations and accepts compromises, so that an idealist need not be a perfectionist or a purist contemptuous of any society that is not as perfect or coherent as a work of art. Again, one could show that ideals and interests do not represent two different *levels* at which a moral and political argument is conducted but rather its two interacting and complementary *dimensions*. But let us concentrate on Hare's distinction between ideals and interests and the paradox it creates.

Hare tends to assume that an interest is the satisfaction of a felt want, and that a man's interest consists in the satisfaction of his wants. But surely it is possible to ask if what you want is really in your interest. You may like walking, but your wife might ask if it is in your interest to go out for a walk when you are ill. Or you may enjoy smoking, but I may ask if it is in your interest to do so when you are suffering from tuberculosis. Interests are not pre-moral or natural entities as Hare assumes, and ideals of physical or moral well-being enter into their very definition.

Conversely, ideals are not some hypothetical and ethereal entities, but conditions of life believed to be good. To suggest that health or justice or equality is an ideal is to indicate no more than that it would promote the *interest* of human beings if they were healthy or were given opportunities that were their due. Morality cannot be defined as the pursuit of others' interests, for the simple reason that these interests themselves are defined and determined by morality. And it cannot be argued[1] either that moral rules must be in the interest of or for the good of all, for the simple reason that the interest or good of the individual cannot be defined independently of moral rules.

Hare's distinction creates an interesting paradox. As a moral being, I have a duty to relieve your suffering and to help you within the limits of my abilities and other obligations. I remain responsible for my actions, and I cannot abdicate that responsibility. It is I who has to live with my actions, and therefore I must be convinced that what I am doing is right. This means that I simply cannot accept your statement of your wants as the sole determinant of my action. I need to be convinced that your wants are morally approvable, and that in satisfying them I am not being an accomplice to an immoral deed. Thus ultimately it is by *my* conception of your good that my action is determined. Besides, your wants may be many and I cannot possibly satisfy them all, and in any case I need to

[1] Both Strawson and Baier come close to saying this. G. Wallace and A. D. M. Walker (eds.), *The Definition of Morality* (Methuen, 1970), pp. 108 f., 199f., and 205.

compare their moral urgency against those of others who too have a moral claim on me. Therefore I need not only to *judge* but also to *grade* them, and this can be done not on the basis of a computerized calculation of the preferences of the parties involved but only on the basis of my moral values. To put the point differently, to the extent that you need my co-operation I cannot but demand a share, however minimal, in deciding how you should live your life, and being moral involves judging your interests by my ideals before I decide to promote them. In requiring me simply to promote your interests as *you* define them, Hare is urging me to bow unquestioningly to the facticity of your interests and to abdicate my moral responsibility for my own actions!

The paradox is resoluble only if it is assumed that your values are more or less the same as mine, so that you would claim nothing as your interest that I cannot approve. That is to say, Hare's moral theory is practicable only in a relatively homogeneous society with generally agreed moral standards,[1] which is strange in someone who enshrines the principle of universalization in the very heart of his moral theory. Hare's distinction between ideal and interest is a modified version of the all-too-familiar positivist distinction between fact and value, and is open to the same familiar objections some of which we have considered above.

Like many Liberal moral philosophers, Hare is impaled on the horns of a dilemma. In my relation with you, am I to promote your interest as you define it? Or as I define it? If the former, then I am abdicating my responsibility for my actions, and this the Liberal cannot want. If the latter, then I am not accepting you as the best judge of your interest and I am setting myself up as your guardian, and this too the Liberal cannot want. As a good moral philosopher, Hare knows the first position is clearly untenable, since people can be mistaken in their judgement of their interests. Indeed, he even says that the 'opinion of the majority proves nothing in moral questions'.[2] He would also restrain drug addicts because 'we do have an ideal of the good man and the good society such that it cannot be realized by a drug addict or by a society which contains such men'.[3]

This is fine, but it means that Hare is now rejecting his earlier conception of interest since he is now deciding what the *real* interest of the addict is. Hare is also rejecting the basic Liberal premise that every man is the best judge of his own interest. He does not realize, further, that his

[1] 'And it has been the mark of all these philosophers that they have been extremely conventional; they have nothing in them by which to revolt against the conventional standards of their sort of people; it is impossible that they should be profound.' G. E. M. Anscombe in *The Definition of Morality*, op. cit., p. 226.
[2] ibid., p. 174.
[3] ibid., p. 175.

discussion of drug addicts opens up a large number of questions. Is there a difference between true and false consciousness? Can a man be seriously mistaken in his conception of his wants? Could some grown-ups be really like children? Can a whole way of life rest on some fundamental misunderstanding of human nature? These questions, vital to Hare's discussion, cannot be answered except with the help of a substantive conception of man – the task that Hare has explicitly abjured on the basis of a mistaken conception of the nature of philosophy.

We saw earlier that an impartial consideration of others' interests is an essential element in moral consciousness.[1] But here again positivism has mutilated the full force of the principle of impartiality. In considering how my action affects your interests I may simply take account of your interests as they pertain to you in your given condition, and may not inquire if it can be impartially justified that you should be in that condition in the first instance. Thus I am being impartial in commending a good man and condemning a criminal. But if I do not ask why he should have become a criminal, if his poverty and bad family life are to be blamed, and if society has been unfair to him, I am tolerating partiality at a deeper level. Or again, I am applying the principle of equal opportunity impartially when I decide that an intelligent child should be given certain opportunities that cannot be given to a less intelligent child. But as I am accepting the fact of their differences as given and unalterable, and as I am not inquiring if the less intelligent child can be helped to become more intelligent or if human capacities cannot be raised over the course of generations, my undoubtedly genuine impartiality at one level conceals profound partiality at a deeper level. The fact of the inequality of intelligence is not in doubt; what is in dispute is our response to it. Are we to accept the inequality as a datum without any further inquiry and construct our social institutions on that basis, or are we to ask ourselves if something can and should be done about it, if the inequality can and should be reduced, if all men can be enabled to enjoy the best that human civilization has to offer? The first is a positivist response and, although it pretends to be realistic and scientific, its reasons for treating as immutable what can be and has been empirically shown to be changeable and its refusal to go behind facts and evaluate them are ideologically inspired and have no objective basis.

This tendency to accept a prevailing condition as a natural fact and the resulting failure to see its historicity and mutability, which is what I mean by positivism here, has misled moral philosophy in a number of ways. It is generally the lowest common denominator or what appears to be common to most men that has been taken as a factual basis of society.

[1] W. F. Frankena, 'The Concept of Morality', in *The Definition of Morality*, op. cit., p. 172.

LIBERALISM AND MORALITY

In moral psychology this has led to the view that the individual is essentially self-centred, and it is therefore taken to be a serious philosophical problem to show why he should be moral and do what is right. Now, surely, this is a pseudo-problem since one should have thought that being moral involves doing what is right, and that the right should be done simply because it is right. Of course moral situations are rarely clear-cut, and one needs to inquire what is the right thing to do; but once the moral agent has concluded that he ought to act in a particular way, there can be no further question as to why he should do it. It is only the creature whose sole point of reference is his own subjectivity and who has not yet acquired a capacity for objective existence, for self-transcendence, who would dream of asking 'that old philosophical question',[1] as to how morality can be shown to pay or what motive he can have for behaving morally. As a rational being I need to have a reason for my actions, but the reason does not have to be anything other than the fact that this is my duty, that it is right. I may be a type of person who has not yet learnt to be guided by the objective considerations of what is right, in which case I need to be morally educated, both in the sense of being made aware of what being moral involves, and being made more sensitive and imaginative. The answer, that is to say, is not to accept my self-centredness as a fact and pander to it by showing that morality is in my interest or that the right is only another name for self-interest, but instead to release me from, to draw me out of, my subjective framework and to get me to act on objective and impersonal motives.

The same positivist tendency reappears in the doctrine that 'ought' implies 'can'.[2] It is trivially true that one cannot be expected to do something that one is simply incapable of doing. There is no point in telling a person that he ought to help a man in distress when he cannot walk or see or is seriously ill or is in some way physically incapacitated. But this is not how this dictum has been always interpreted. Once the concept of 'can' is taken out of the physical and psychological realm where one can clearly determine what is and what is not possible, and is applied to other areas where this is not possible to determine, there is a danger of erecting contingencies into eternal verities. Human conduct is so much a matter of belief and opinion that there is almost nothing men cannot do if they come to believe that it is right. There are men who eat nothing

---

[1] F. F. Strawson, 'Social Morality and Individual Ideal', in *The Definition of Morality*, op. cit., p. 106.
[2] The opposite dictum that 'can' implies 'ought', that whatever can be should be produced, invented, created, is no less positivist, and is indeed the inspiring principle of the technological society as Galbraith has shown in his *The New Industrial State*.

but meat because they believe it is good for their health; and there are others who are sickened by its sight because they feel revolted by the violence it involves. If we thought that adultery was a mortal sin, we could so socialize and condition our children that over the course of generations the very concept of adultery might disappear from their vocabulary. After all, the acute social conditioning in many parts of Asia and Africa has made premarital sex a rarity. The question then is to *decide* where we are to draw the line of 'can', and the sensible way to answer it is to inquire what men today are capable of doing, whether we think they ought to develop new capacities and sensitivities and how we can help them acquire them.

What has happened, in fact, is different. Moral philosophers have simply accepted certain 'facts' as facts of human nature. Thus H. L. A. Hart takes it as one of the basic facts about men that they are selfish and have limited sympathies, and that therefore we should not ask them to do things involving sacrifices of their interests.[1] In trimming morality to conform to 'facts', he avoids the basic issue whether these 'facts' are really facts of human nature or whether they are 'facts' only within a particular social context that depends on and therefore constantly reinforces human selfishness as its principle of motion.

Perhaps Hart is right that man really is and cannot but behave as he describes him, but surely that needs to be shown and not simply assumed or asserted. Though controversial, it is not prima facie implausible to argue that man has no nature and that all his thoughts, feelings and responses are results of long social acculturation over several generations. This would suggest that although there are therefore *historical* facts about men, there are no *natural* facts, and that historical facts by definition can be changed, modified, transformed if we once decide that they ought to be. What is called human 'nature' is really a cultural product, and man is ultimately his own artifact. And therefore while it is true that moral norms must take account of human beings as they are at any given time, it is no less true that we ought to evaluate morally the historical human condition itself and inquire if we ought not to change it and how. The relationship between 'ought' and 'can' is far more complex than is suggested by the one-sided doctrine that 'ought' implies 'can'. 'Ought' is as much limited by 'can' as 'can' is by 'ought'.

III

We explored in the first two sections some of the basic characteristics of Liberal morality and concluded that it is inadequate. We saw that morality can never be exhausted in the discharge of the duties and

[1] *The Concept of Law* (Oxford, 1961), p. 189 f.

obligations one has consciously undertaken; it is concerned with alleviating suffering as well. We also saw that morality is concerned with alleviating not merely physical suffering but also other types of suffering; that it is not merely concerned with alleviating them but also with preventing them; that it is not merely concerned with preventing suffering but also with positively helping others to live a good life; that it does not meekly accept a prevailing condition of life but inquires if it is just, fair, good and if it should be changed.

Though we have not argued it explicitly, we have implied in our critique of the Liberal morality that morality is nothing if not an acceptance of the other person at least as an equal. When confronted with another person one can respond to him in one of three ways. One can either treat him as a mere means to one's interests; or one can treat him as a locus of claims like oneself and thus morally one's equal; or one can treat his claims as superior to one's own. The first understood either as universalized egoism or as solipsistic egoism is not a moral attitude at all and is open to a number of fatal objections so acutely analysed by Moore, Baier and others. It is only the second that marks the emergence of morality proper. The third is an attitude of altruism. Whether or not altruism represents a higher morality, it is clear that morality requires, minimally, the recognition of the other person as an equal, as someone entitled to conditions of good life in a way that one considers oneself entitled, as a person with hopes, desires, potentialities.

The full force of this fundamental moral truth is constantly blunted by our self-absorbed pursuit of our self-concerned goals, that generates merely an external awareness of the presence of others, much as if they were things or, at best, no more than a human background to our existence. But once one has grasped the full truth of the recognition of the other as a person and a fully moral consciousness has emerged, one begins to feel concerned about him – about the way he lives, the way he is treated by others, the opportunities that life and society have to offer him. Such a fully developed moral consciousness can no longer be content to remain a sentimental nurse-maid nobly but pathetically dedicated to healing wounds, but generates a tough-minded and masculine refusal to put up with a condition of life that is unjust, unfair or inhuman and that starves human beings, or confines them to a life of dull and joyless drudgery, or sentences them to a life haunted by bleak despair.

When morality is conceived, as properly speaking it must be, on these positive, radical and universalist lines, it becomes a radical pursuit of a just society committed to the realization of the conditions of good life for all its members. In other words, morality then becomes political, politics now seen, as indeed it must be, as a medium through which to express one's concern for one's fellow men and to strive to achieve a good society. In withdrawing morality from the public world where it is needed most and confining it to the cosy world of interpersonal relations,[1] and in thus restricting its scope and impact, the Liberal is in danger, paradoxically, of moralizing morality out of existence.

[1] *Principia Ethica,* op. cit., p. 188f., where it is concluded after a clever but disappointing investigation that personal affection and enjoyment of beauty are the two highest goods.

An International Morality?

GEOFFREY GOODWIN

'Peace must be founded .... if it is not to fail, upon the intellectual and moral superiority of mankind.'
UNESCO Constitution

'Morality is a function of the struggle of the proletariat.'
Lenin

'To this war of every man, against every man, this also is consequent, that nothing can be unjust. Notions of right and wrong, justice and injustice have there no place.'
Hobbes

The Covenant of the League of Nations and the Charter of the United Nations both assumed, as did the UNESCO Constitution, the relevance of moral norms to international life. Both expressed a moral purpose. The Covenant sought to 'promote open, just and honourable relations between nations'; the Charter, more ambitiously, sought not only to 'save succeeding generations from the scourge of war', but also, *inter alia*, to 'achieve international co-operation in ... promoting and encouraging respect for human rights and for fundamental freedoms for all without distinction as to race, sex, language or religion' (Article 1 [3]).

Both the Covenant and the Charter reflected, and were initially sustained by, the widespread sense of revulsion evoked by the appalling savagery of two world wars, which seemed to demonstrate beyond doubt the need for moral restraints on the behaviour of states. Yet as the memories of war receded, so did the moral norms they expressed come to be questioned. To the revisionist Axis powers in the 1930s the precepts of the Covenant were but a hypocritical gloss on the interests of the *status quo* powers in sustaining the 'diktat' of Versailles. To the Communist world they were an emanation of an outdated and discredited bourgeois capitalist morality. To many non-European peoples today many of the Purposes and Principles of the Charter are redolent of the political vocabulary of a Western world from which they have liberated, or seek to liberate, themselves.

At the United Nations the often ostentatious public expressions of deference to the Purposes and Principles of the Charter seem to bear little relevance to the actual practice of member states. The 'great wild-goose chase', as Herbert Nicholas has called it, to protect the individual and his rights, has often been tragically matched by a flagrant disregard for those rights or by the disposition of many governments to exploit them for 'cold war' or 'anti-colonial' purposes. A certain regard for the injunction against 'the threat or use of force' (Article 2 [4]) between states is matched by the frequency with which force is used, whether within states to check secessionist movements, or to subdue political or religious minorities, or to subvert colonialist or racist regimes. Indeed, at times it seems to be the moral pretensions of nations, rather than their genuine deference to any overriding moral code, which threatens to make this century not only the age of conflict, but also the age of self-righteous and moralist intolerance.

Does this mean that the public deference to the moral norms set out in the Charter and elsewhere is no more than part of the rhetoric of diplomacy based primarily on considerations of diplomatic prudence – for instance, that a reputation for moral rectitude might turn out to be a diplomatic asset – or on calculations of political expediency – namely, the desire to avoid domestic political criticism of an apparent transgression of the moral law? Or do the antics of self-justification in which states are apt to indulge when they are charged with ignoring these norms indicate a genuine recognition of their validity and a desire at least to approximate towards them in so far as political necessity allows? And, indeed, what do we mean when we use the term 'international morality'? Do we mean no more than the diplomatic *mores* of international society,[1] a deference to which, in utilitarian fashion and on a strictly reciprocal basis, is seen as a necessary basis for any international order? Or have we in mind also the notion of an international morality which reflects, however imperfectly and approximately, moral imperatives which have a universal validity and are not, like diplomatic *mores* peculiar to a particular society at a particular moment of its history? The responses to these questions will, as a matter of convenience, be grouped together in three categories: the moralist, the ideologue, and the realist. The main

[1] For instance, a regard – on a strict basis of reciprocity – for diplomatic conventions – such as diplomatic immunities – for a legal system which can provide a source of order and predictability, or for restraints on the use of force lest, in a nuclear age, it prove mutually destructive.

AN INTERNATIONAL MORALITY?

features of each will be outlined below, although, it must be stressed, in necessarily simplistic and stereotyped terms.

The Moralist

The Moralist outlook is most deeply embedded in the Anglo–American tradition of international thought. It is characterized by the belief in the existence of universally valid moral – and legal – principles, rooted in an absolute ethic, and perceptible through reason – or faith – these principles being held valid among all men at all times and in all places. Moreover, they are seen as directly applicable to international political life. They are, as has been said, reflected directly in the principles accepted by members of the United Nations of equal political rights, equal economic opportunities, the rule of law, and the outlawry of the use of force, 'save in the common interest'.

It is these principles, rather than practice or historical experience, which the moralist asserts will increasingly afford the most reliable guide to political action. Thus, Woodrow Wilson claimed that 'Selfish national purposes were being supplanted by universal principles of mankind'. And it is to be noted that moralist doctrine, like rationalist doctrine, does not ask, as Hedley Bull once remarked, 'what principles are, in fact, in practice recognized by international society at a particular time, rather it postulates principles which ought to be recognized by that society at any time.' The stress, then, is on what states *ought* to do – and ought not to do – rather than on what states *actually* do. But there is the conviction that most states most of the time do conform to these moral precepts, not merely because they recognize it to be expedient to do so, but out of a genuine recognition of their obligatory character. 'This proposition [Fiat justitia, pereat mundus] just means that political maxims must not start from the prosperity and happiness that are to be expected in each State from following them; ... but they must proceed from the pure conception of the duty of Right or Justice, as an obligatory principle given *a priori* by pure reason. And this is to be held whatever may be the physical consequences which follow from adopting these political principles.'[1]

One of the underlying assumptions of the moralist school is that the society of states constitutes, in Tonnies' term, a *Gemeinschaft*, that is, a closely knit community exhibiting a high degree of solidarity and a genuine sense of moral purpose. The notion of an international community may be only feebly and somewhat fitfully reflected in the behaviour of

[1] M. G. Forsyth, H. M. A. Keens-Soper, P. Savigear (eds.), *The Theory of International Relations*, Immanuel Kant, Extract 3, *Perpetual Peace: A Philosophical Essay*, Appendix (Unwin University Books, 1970), p. 236.

states, but it nevertheless constitutes, it is held, one of those great civilizing ideas which informs the behaviour of states. Moreover, it is argued that all the advances of recent years are tending to make that community increasingly closely knit, not only technologically but also psychologically. The consequent keener sense of moral responsibility of states is increasingly to be seen both in the field of disaster relief and in their readiness to adhere to conventions outlawing genocide or racial discrimination or embodying political as well as economic and social human rights. There is also reflected here, it is asserted, not only the notion of an international or intergovernmental community, but that of a community of mankind, 'latent, half-glimpsed, and groping for its necessary fulfilment' (Dante), made up not of states but of the individual men, women and children of flesh and blood that people them. The preoccupation of the United Nations with human rights, with social welfare in, for instance, the care of refugees, as well as the earlier attempts of the League of Nations to eradicate slavery or the traffic in women and children, are all held to illustrate the growing moral concern of the international community for the plight and rights of the individual.

The corollary of the notion of the moral responsibility of states and of the belief in an absolute morality valid for all times and all places is the conviction that, in Woodrow Wilson's terms, 'the same standards of morality should apply to states as apply to individuals'. In other words, there is the denial of the notion of a 'dual morality', that is, one moral code for states and another for individuals, and there is the belief, affirmed indeed in the Nuremberg Tribunal and in the Tokyo War Crimes Tribunal, that the individual cannot plead necessity of state or superior orders as an excuse for the committal of crimes against humanity.

The belief in natural law, in a system of eternal and immutable principles radiating from some transcendent authority and which are expressed, albeit in approximate terms, in much of international law, is also integral to moralist thought, which places a good deal of stress on the norm-setting role of international law. Indeed, one of the main aims of moralists is to give moral precepts legal status in the hope that thereby they will become more effectively binding on the behaviour of states. The underlying premise of international law, *pacta sunt servanda*, is seen as a moral one, and the main sanction behind it is seen as public opinion. Cobden held that the enlightened opinion of mankind would become so hostile to war that in the end 'states will all turn moralists in self-defence'. Or, as Woodrow Wilson claimed: 'We are depending primarily and chiefly on one great force, that is the moral force of the public opinion of the world, the cleansing and clarifying and compelling influences of publicity.' In this Wilsonian tradition world opinion – in what was in 1919 expected to be a mainly democratic world – was assumed almost

AN INTERNATIONAL MORALITY?

unquestioningly to be mainly peace-loving and therefore ready to exercise its voice in favour of peace. To do so, however, it had to be fully informed of all events in the international sphere so that the 'conscience of mankind' could properly exercise its authority; hence the call for 'open covenants, openly arrived at'.

The moralist, then, is concerned with what states *ought* to do in terms not merely of the diplomatic mores of international society at a particular moment in its history which it is convenient for states to observe on a reciprocal basis, but rather of moral imperatives which it is incumbent on members of that society, both states and individuals, to adhere to. Thus the obligations of the Covenant of the League of Nations against the illegal use of force were held to be directly operative on the conscience of member states which, in the event of their violation, would react spontaneously against the wrongdoer, under Article 16. And if it be pointed out that what states actually do bears little relation to what the moralist thinks they ought to do, the reply more often than not will be that it is state behaviour that must be changed rather than that the moral precepts must be diluted to approximate more closely to that behaviour. If unhappily the performance of members of the United Nations did not match up to the principles they professed to accept, this, Dag Hammarskjöld asserted, was no argument for abandoning 'the clear approach of the Charter ... Rather ... member nations jointly should increase their efforts to make political realities gradually come closer to the pattern established by the Charter.'[1]

In criticism, it can be said that the moralist is far too apt to suffer from the *hubris* of assuming that his principles are without question universally valid and generally applicable when they may only be very relative and, indeed, subjective. Wilson's: 'I speak for humanity' is but one example of this nationalistic universalism which projects on to the international stage the principles held dear by a particular national leader.[2] The moralist continually risks encapsulating the complexities of international life into simple formulae in an attempt to secure clear-cut answers to moral questions.

Thus much of moralist thinking about the 'illegal' use of force wrongly assumes the moral clarity of situations in which force is used. Or there is the tragic disposition to assume that if force is used in a 'just' cause it is more important that it should emerge triumphant than that it

---

[1] Dag Hammarskjöld, Introduction to the Annual Report of the Secretary-General on the work of the Organization, 16 June 1960–15 June 1961, reprinted in *International Organization*, Autumn 1961, p. 556.

[2] It is fair to recall, however, Sir Denis Brogan's apt epitaph on – and tribute to – Woodrow Wilson: 'Wilson stood for human decency; he stood weakly, but he stood where it is good to stand.'

should be conducted by means which keep human suffering to a minimum and which hold open the possibilities for negotiation. To the moralist the just use of force only too often appears as a form of punishment against the criminal aggressor – aggression being a sin or a crime to be expiated – the unconditional surrender of the criminal being therefore the ultimate aim rather than an earlier negotiated end to the fighting. There is, unhappily, more than a grain of truth in A. J. P. Taylor's bitter comment that: 'Bismarck fought "necessary" wars and killed thousands; the idealists of the Twentieth Century fight "just" wars and kill millions.'

There is the further danger that the preoccupation with human rights, and in particular with racial discrimination and its eradication, will incite forcible intervention – and possible counter-intervention – in the internal affairs of those states alleged to be infringing those rights, leading thereby to greater human suffering than already exists. Fundamentally, however, it is the notion of the moral solidarity of mankind which is at issue. Is it not rather the case that international society is becoming increasingly atomized, not only politically but also culturally and morally? If so, may not pretensions to moral universalism be a more serious threat to the delicate fabric of that society – and, indeed, in a nuclear age a threat to its very survival – than the kind of moral relativism that moralists so abhor?

The Ideologues
Moralists look to a millennium in which moral principles of 'peace' and 'justice' will more effectively govern the practices of states; but it will be an *internationalist* millennium, that is, a millennium in which sovereign states will continue to exist, even though they will co-exist not in a virtual state of anarchy, but in an effectively functioning world community. The ideologues of the Communist persuasion seek, of course, radically to transform the present international society. Their moral goal is to refashion the world in the image of the proletariat. There is a vision here of ultimate goals and an abiding faith in their inevitable attainment. Progress towards social justice lies in that which helps, retrogression in that which hinders, the socialist revolution of the proletariat, for, as Marx put it, 'real social justice can only come in the last stages of Communism'. The principle of proletarian cosmopolitanism is, therefore, as Engels put it, 'superior to all your (bourgeois) codes and mores'.

In Communist ideology, 'morality is a function of the struggle of the proletariat' (Lenin) – that which hastens the victory of the proletariat is morally right, that which impedes it is morally wrong. In other words, 'Everything is right which serves the revolution.' The end does, indeed, justify the means. Notions of revolutionary justice are, therefore, in large measure a function of the needs of the proletarian revolution. This, in turn, usually implies not only support for liberation movements struggling against capitalist imperialists, but also the paramount importance of the security and solidarity of the socialist camp as a base for further revolutionary advances. The logical corollary is that no socialist state can be an aggressor, or an imperialist, or infringe human rights, as these delinquencies are attributes of non-socialist, bourgeois capitalist states.

Marxist ideology is universalist in its claims. It postulates the absolute unity of mankind as an ideal; as yet there is only potential solidarity, but full solidarity will be realized when the proletarian revolution has triumphed. Meanwhile the revolutionary struggle – the basic struggle is between classes rather than between states – is one. 'Today's revolution is one, its goals and its techniques are everywhere similar, the goal being to overthrow world capitalist imperialism' (Mao Tse Tung). Moreover, although tactically the attainment of these long-term goals has had to be adapted of recent years to the existing balances of forces in the world, particularly in a nuclear world, so as to dictate a policy of 'peaceful coexistence of countries with differing social systems', that coexistence is seen as only a transitory phase. Nor does it mean 'conciliation of the socialist and bourgeois ideologies. On the contrary it implies intensification of the struggle of the working class, of all the communist parties for the triumph of socialist ideas.'[1] That struggle, whether by the property-less against the property-owning or by indigenous liberation movements against colonial rulers, is represented as that of the new and progressive against the old and moribund; the only qualification, though an important one, is that to minimize the risks of a nuclear confrontation, the struggle between the two main camps is at present to be conducted almost exclusively by peaceful means. The necessities of survival condition the ideological imperatives.

Quite logically, there is little place in this ideology for the concepts of 'justice' embodied in traditional notions of 'natural law' or in the 'general principles of international law recognized by civilized nations' (Article 38 [c] of the Statute of the International Court of Justice). For the most part a strictly positivistic view is taken of general international law and, since the latter is seen as based on the doctrine of peaceful coexistence, it is supposed that it can last only so long as the latter prevails. Nor does the notion of 'good faith', of *pacta sunt servanda*, seem to have much place in Communist doctrine; a regard for legal obligations is a matter of reciprocal convenience or interest and, at least in

[1] Statement of the Conference of Eighty-one Communist and Workers' Parties, Moscow, 6 December 1960, in *Documents on International Affairs, 1960* (O.U.P. for R.I.I.A., 1964), p. 229.

doctrine, is tempered by the belief that 'with (bourgeois) heretics there is no need to keep faith'.[1]

Moreover, in Communist doctrine there are two systems of international law. The one is general international law between differing social systems, the other is represented by treaties, etc., amongst the socialist states. This latter system is seen as one based not merely on the principle of coexistence, but on the higher level of 'Marxist-Leninist principles of proletarian internationalism'. These principles, it is claimed, provide the foundation for 'the birth of socialist international law of future humanity liberated from capitalist slavery'. In consequence, socialist international law takes precedence over general international law; and in the event of a conflict of laws, relations between socialist states are not to be seen as subject to the obligations of the general system of international law; they are the province of this newly emerging and superior system of international socialist law.[2]

In Communist ideology little importance also seems to be attached to that part of international law designed to improve the lot of the individual. Indeed, the whole notion of the innate rights of the individual has little place in that ideology. Man is seen as essentially a social being who derives his rights from society. Those rights will therefore most effectively be enlarged by the achievement of a classless society in which his sense of 'alienation' will finally be resolved.

The Soviet Union may still claim to be 'the only fatherland of the world proletariat', but Soviet tactics in seeking the proletarian millennium have been for the most part cautious and pragmatic and have portrayed a keen sense of the limitations imposed, as well as of the opportunities afforded, by the balance of forces existing at a particular moment in history. Indeed, at times Soviet practice has conformed so closely to traditionalist notions of great power behaviour as to call into question whether it has not lost altogether its revolutionary commitment – as, indeed, the Chinese claim. Although the system of values reflected in the goals of the proletarian revolution is still publicly affirmed and the perceptions of Soviet leaders still appear to be coloured to some extent by their ideological preconceptions and values,

---

[1] Compare the Council of Constance's (1415) decision to burn John Huss, in disregard of earlier undertakings, on the grounds that 'cum hereticis fides non servanda'.

[2] A logical corollary of this reasoning being the Brezhnev doctrine of 'limited sovereignty'. The reasoning is not altogether novel. Compare the *inter se* doctrine in Commonwealth practice (the view until recently, that is, that relations between members of the Commonwealth were different in kind from ordinary international relations); or the principle in the Rome Treaty that European Community Law takes precedence over Municipal Law within the Six.

AN INTERNATIONAL MORALITY?

there is a good deal of evidence to suggest that ideological ties have become mainly instrumental (for example, they are to be seen mainly in terms of the control over most communist parties exercised by the Communist Party of the Soviet Union, a control which reflects more immediately the interests of the Soviet Union than of the class struggle). If so, the ability of international society to assimilate revolutionary powers has once again been strikingly demonstrated. In the process, revolutionary values may become increasingly overlaid by the conventional *mores* of international society. The modes of behaviour – for instance the inhibitions on the use of force – induced initially by the temporary demands of peaceful coexistence may begin to strike deeper roots and even in time acquire a moral status not dissimilar to that implied in the Charter. Political values can sometimes acquire real binding force even when their first roots are struck in calculations of political expediency.

It is this process of assimilation to which Mao Tse Tung has taken such exception. For Mao Tse Tung doctrinal purity is both a moral imperative as a safeguard against the corrupting influence of bourgeois revisionism and bureaucratic routinization and a guide and measure of political behaviour. He continues to assert the absolute moral validity of the Marxist–Leninist doctrine and its direct applicability to political action. Moreover, the traditional Chinese view of the world, which sees China as the centre, the sole upholder of true civilization, the lawgiver to the barbarians, makes conformity with the traditional *mores* of the former Western-dominated international society peculiarly difficult.

Yet there are signs that even here the process of assimilation is already at work. This, of course, may only reflect a tactical reappraisal on the Chinese part of the existing balance of forces in the world at large. But the Chinese desire to restore conventional diplomatic relations with the outside world and to secure a seat in the United Nations has already brought some softening of revolutionary militancy. Whether Communist China's presence within the United Nations system may lead her to adopt some of the conventional *mores* – even values – of that system or whether her main object is to secure a refashioning of the system itself in line with revolutionary requirements remains, of course, to be seen.

If the latter is China's aim she can be expected to find ready allies amongst several of the more ideologically inclined Afro–Asian leaders in the General Assembly of the United Nations whose notions of revolutionary justice have come increasingly to dominate that body. Conor Cruise O'Brien has rightly said that where colonial and racist issues are involved 'the tendency of the majority of the United Nations is to pursue justice at some risk of war'. Indeed, to many of its

Afro–Asian and some of its Latin–American members the United Nations is seen as an instrument of justice rather than as an instrument of order – justice here being defined mainly in terms of the elimination of all forms of racial discrimination (at least by whites against non-whites) and of any remaining traces of colonialism or neo-colonialism.

One consequence is that much of the more ideologically oriented anti-colonialist thinking is impregnated with the concept of the 'just' war. Thus, the conflicts in Algeria or Southern Africa have been seen as primarily 'wars of liberation', as 'just' wars which are in conformity with the Purposes and Principles of the Charter and therefore not at variance with the prohibitions of Article 2 (4) of the Charter. As Mr Krishna Menon put it at the time of the Indian occupation of Goa in December 1961: 'We consider colonialism is permanent aggression. . . . We did not commit aggression. Colonialism collapsed.'

Colonialism is not only denounced as an anachronism and an affront to human dignity, but it is conveniently forgotten that it often brought a degree of order to dependent peoples which many successor regimes have failed to match. Most Afro–Asian states would argue that military intervention in Angola or Mozambique does not constitute aggression against Portugal, as the latter has already unjustly embarked on an oppressive colonial war against the African peoples of those territories. Similarly, apartheid is seen as a form of war against the black African peoples of South Africa which justifies armed intervention on their behalf. The same considerations apply to the illegal white racist minority regime in Zimbabwe (Rhodesia). In the case of Namibia (South-West Africa), indeed, the United Nations is seen as having a direct responsibility for enforcing its authority – if necessary by physical force – in a territory in which the Union of South Africa is alleged to have forfeited its right to exercise its mandate. That the just use of force to liberate these territories may seriously threaten international order and indeed cause even greater suffering to the inhabitants is not thought to denigrate from the moral imperative to realize the dictates of justice.

Moreover, to the most militant anti-colonialists violence itself is seen as not only a unifying force, but as a cleansing and purifying force which can help to 'tear the mask of hypocrisy from the face of the enemy'.[1] Violence, indeed, is seen as a necessary instrument for the eradication of injustice and for the pursuit of progress.

Appeals to international law are also apt to fall on deaf ears. The obligations of international law are seen primarily as a derogation from some higher principle of international justice, in particular, the principle of national self-determination. Indeed, much of the content of present-

[1] Hannah Arendt, *On Violence* (Penguin Press, 1970), pp. 65–6.

day international law is thought to reflect the interests of, and so to operate primarily as an instrument of, the *status quo* colonial powers; it therefore is thought to have little or no moral status. There is, indeed, a strong sense of the hypocrisy and self-righteousness of the colonial powers and therefore a tendency to reject the values that they profess. As Professor Martin Wight once put it, they are pictured as 'once the burglars, now on the magistrates' bench'.

What anti-colonialist ideologues seek is to turn the moral injunctions of those Purposes and Principles of the Charter on which they lay particular stress (for instance, human rights) into legal form. Thus they have sought to give the principle of self-determination of peoples legal status through Declaration 1514 of 14 December 1960 on the granting of independence to colonial countries and peoples. This Declaration, by lending precision to Article 1 (2) of the Charter – which enjoins 'respect for the principle of equal rights and self-determination of peoples' – attempted to set out a binding law which could be held in effect to legitimize the collective use of force against recalcitrant colonial powers. Similarly, they have sought in the Convention on the Elimination of all Forms of Racial Discrimination to codify in legal form the fundamental freedom enunciated in Article 1 (3) of the Charter, and by so doing to provide a legal basis for collective action against racist regimes.

In the economic sphere many have asserted that economic aid should be seen as a form of restitution for past economic exploitation of their resources and they have asserted their permanent sovereignty over natural resources in their territories, both as a moral right and as a means of safeguarding those resources against what they allege to be neo-colonialist exploitation.

These attempts to enunciate new norms of international behaviour reflecting the 'just' claims of newly emerging states, should not be regarded solely as part of the rhetoric of international debate. It is true that their validity is often questionable, that their realization is closely circumscribed by the limited capacities of their protagonists and that the bargaining power of those who profess them is, in the context of great power relations, declining. Yet the more militant Afro-Asian ideologues have been instrumental in projecting into United Nations discussions their own system of values to the point where the organization no longer reflects, as for the most part it did at its inception, the political vocabulary of the West in terms both of the values which form part of the political heritage of the West and of the norms which animate most democratic forms of government in the Western World. In the process the United Nations has become a more pluralistic, or rather, atomized body. The preoccupation with justice rather than order, with rights rather than obligations, has inevitably weakened any remaining moral concensus behind the principles and purposes of the Charter, but one result is that it has come to reflect more closely the realities of international life.

The Realists
These realities are, for the realist, the political atomization of contemporary international society following the dismantling of Western European empires, the growing cultural pluralism as indigenous cultures have broken through the often thin veneer of Western imperial civilization, and the continuing, though possibly declining, significance of ideological differences; all of which are held to confirm the continued absence of any true sense of international community, and therefore to cast doubts on the existence of any generally accepted code of international morality. Far from seeing himself as part of an increasingly self-conscious community of mankind, to most realists man seems locked as firmly as ever in his national cell. Sovereign states are still the main actors and decision-making centres on the international stage, and their decisions still rest mainly on calculations of where their interests lie and the relative power they can muster to pursue them.

Some realists draw the conclusion that moral issues are therefore quite irrelevant to political action in that there are no universally valid moral principles relevant to the behaviour of states. Politics is essentially an amoral activity. Politics is the realm of power, not of morals. The discussion of moral restraints, moral scruples and moral norms is futile and absurd. It is also dangerous, since to rely on the supposed altruism or scruples of others can be a recipe for disaster as well as disillusion. This view, according to Garrett Mattingley, was enunciated quite explicitly by Machiavelli who, he says, held that 'since every state was an autonomous entity, recognizing no superior and no interest higher than its own, no rules of ethics whatever applied to relations between states. The only test was success.'[1] Later, in the *Leviathan*, Hobbes was to write: 'To this war, of every man against every man, this also is consequent, that nothing can be unjust. Notions of right or wrong, justice or injustice have there no place. Where there is no common power, there is no law; where no law, no injustice.'

This view that international politics is basically amoral – and that states' main preoccupation is necessarily with their security – reflects in the case of Hobbes and others the view that the state alone creates morality as well as law. As Hobbes wrote: 'There is neither morality nor law outside the state.' But there is the more dangerous Hegelian view that states are complete and morally self-sufficient entities. Hegel wrote

[1] G. Mattingley, 'Machiavelli' in *The Renaissance* (ed. J. H. Plumb, Collins for Horizon Magazine, 1961), p. 64.

of the state alone as being 'the universe of the ethic' and, indeed, he claimed the state to be 'the realized ethical ideal'. The danger here is that any such state habitually falls into the trap of universalizing, whether consciously or subconsciously, the morality peculiar to itself. In the process, men delude themselves into thinking they are gods and 'inhuman means are justified by the superhuman ends'.[1] This is a feature only too common in contemporary international society where the leading nations 'oppose each other as the standard bearers of moral systems, each of national origin, and each of them claiming to provide universal moral and political standards which all the other nations ought to accept'.[2]

It is this brand of nationalistic universalism which has led many realists to argue that, rather than concentrating on erecting moral norms for governing inter-state behaviour, the urgent need is to curb the moral pretensions of states. International conflict needs to be seen, not in terms of the conflict of good with evil, but as an inescapable part of the human predicament in a society lacking any overall 'common authority to keep them all in awe'. 'Much of the international (or domestic) evil of power is rooted not in the sinfulness of man but in a context, a constellation, a situation, in which even good men are forced to act selfishly or immorally.'[3] Herbert Butterfield reminds us that the tragic element in international conflict is that such conflict is not a simple picture of good men fighting bad; rather we need to appreciate that certain situations can contain the elements of conflict irrespective of any particular wickedness of any of the parties concerned. The very structure of international society produces situations of Hobbesian fear, of an irreducible conflict of power. The tragedy is that conflict is apt to be 'embittered by the heat of moral indignation on both sides, just because each was so conscious of its own rectitude, so enraged with the other for leaving it without any alternative to war.'[4] It is this conflict between 'embattled systems of self-righteousness' which is so disruptive of international order. And it is with the preservation of international order that most realists are mainly concerned.

There are realists, however, who affirm not only the existence, but the relevance to political behaviour, of a transcendental and universal ethic and of the moral principles, such as justice, 'good faith', a recognition of

[1] Eric Voeglin, *The New Science of Politics*, (University of Chicago Press, 1962), p. 169.
[2] Hans Morgenthau in his Introduction to David Mitrany, *A Working Peace System*. Quadrangle Books, 1966.
[3] Stanley H. Hoffman (ed.) *Contemporary Theory in International Relations* (Prentice Hall, 1960), p. 31.
[4] H. Butterfield, 'Tragic Element in Modern Conflict' in *History and Human Relations* (Collins, 1951), p. 21.

people as 'persons' not 'things', to be derived from it; and who see these principles as not only consonant with, but as necessary underpinners of, order. The application of these principles is bound to be relative to time and place, for 'universal moral principles cannot be applied to the actions of states in their abstract universal formulation . . . they must be, as it were, filtered through the concrete circumstances of time and place.'[1] The call, in other words, is for a contextual morality or, as some would prefer, an ethical relativism:[2] we need to consider not only what states *ought* to do, but what they *can* do in terms of their security and the welfare of their peoples. International morality poses, in other words, both ontological and existential issues. Moreover, in a quasi-anarchical international society it must be recognized that the parameters of moral choice are bound to be much more closely circumscribed than in an orderly civil society.

Nevertheless, this school of realists – to which the present writer belongs – does hold that the actions of states are subject to universal moral principles in at least three ways. The first is the requirement of cosmic humility as a check on simplistic or self-righteous moralism. 'To know that states are subject to the moral law is one thing; to pretend to know what is morally required of states in a particular situation is quite another.'[3] The proper choice and application of moral principles is extremely difficult; life usually allows only of an approximation to a principle, while the principles themselves only too often conflict – for instance, peace *or* justice. In politics there can be few clear-cut moral choices, for politics is, indeed, as Reinhold Niebuhr once remarked, 'an area where conscience and power meet, where the ethical and coercive factors of human life inter-penetrate and work out their tentative and uneasy compromises.'[4]

The second is that we should neither overstate nor under-rate the influence of morality on international politics. Given, in Churchill's phrase, 'the moral dignity of the national interest', it is the moral responsibility of the statesman to defend the national interest (in terms of what he deems to be the security of the realm and the welfare of its people) for, as Morgenthau remarks, 'if he does not take care of the national interest, nobody else will'. And this may not infrequently require him to draw a distinction between his own moral sympathies and the political interests which it is his duty to protect. Yet the manner in

[1] H. Morgenthau, *Dilemmas of Politics* (University of Chicago Press, 1958), p. 83.

[2] See, for instance, K. W. Thompson, *Christian Ethics and the Dilemmas of Foreign Policy*. Duke University, 1959.

[3] H. Morgenthau, op. cit., p. 81.

[4] R. Niebuhr, *Moral Man and Immoral Society* (Charles Scribner's Sons, 1932), p. 4.

AN INTERNATIONAL MORALITY?

which he does so and the extent to which he gives due weight to the interests of others is of real moral consequence. Experience, in fact, suggests that probably the majority of statesmen do usually exhibit some moral scruples about the ends they seek or about the means they are prepared to use to reach those ends. It is true that power considerations continually set the limits of choice; and it has to be recognized that the sense of justice of the great is often the best guarantee of a measure of justice for the weak. Nevertheless, a statesman still can be, and often is, guided by the moral precept of the 'lesser evil', that is of choosing that course of action which can be expected to entail the minimum of harm. Were recognition of even this modest precept more widespread, a great deal of human suffering could be relieved.

The third is that international order is itself a value. The features of international society which make for order: diplomatic convention, positive as well as customary international law, the balance of power, have, in a real sense, moral status, if only because a minimum of order is a precondition of some measure of justice. This is not to say that order is necessarily an overriding value. Some concern for justice is also a necessary ingredient of order, while some systems of order, especially at the domestic level, may be so oppressive and unjust as to warrant their overthrow. Yet, at the international level, the risks, particularly in a nuclear age, of subordinating the requirements of order to the dictates of justice – and for whom? – are so great as to call for the utmost caution. Such 'minimal order' as does already exist could only too easily be shattered by the demands – usually conflicting – for some 'optimal order' and the world relapse into a state of utter anarchy in which only the strong could survive.

In a world, therefore, where the minimal element of order is so precariously based and where even mankind's survival may be at stake, moral principles need to be weighed against the moral requirements of concrete political action, so that their relative merits can be decided by a prudential evaluation of the political consequences to which they are likely to lead. 'In classic and Christian ethics the first of the moral virtues is *sophia* or *prudentia*, because without adequate understanding of the structure of humanity, including the *conditio humana*, moral action with rational co-ordination of means and ends is hardly possible.'[1] In a nuclear world prudence is still a moral virtue and it is now a recipe for survival.

[1] Eric Voeglin, op. cit., p. 165.

The Machiavellianism of the Machiavellians

GERAINT PARRY

In the early 1940s James Burnham published two works which made both a popular and an academic impact. They combined polemic with theoretical analysis. Both works reflected on contemporaneous political experience and related this experience to the political and social theory of the past. Both, in differing degrees, have given rise to controversy.

The title of the first of these books, *The Managerial Revolution*,[1] gave wide currency to a phrase which has by now become a 'term of art' in politics and political science and in economic affairs and economic studies. Major studies were undertaken which examined the claims put forward by Burnham that a radical transformation, amounting to a revolution, had taken place in the economic structure of modern society, as a result of which a managerial class had displaced the finance capitalist class as the controller of modern industry. The outcome of the debate is still not entirely clear for conceptual and technical reasons, but there would be a large measure of agreement that there has been at least a managerial 'evolution' if not a 'revolution'.[2] As late as 1957 the British Labour Party published a policy statement (*Industry and Society*) on the relation between the state and private industry which was explicitly based upon the Burnhamite thesis and which served to revive the issue.

The title of the second book, *The Machiavellians*,[3] again achieved a certain currency, but this time among a narrower circle of professional political and social theorists. In this work Burnham applied the term 'Machiavellians' to designate a group of political theorists as a school. Burnham was, of course, far from being the first author to apply the

[1] Putnam, New York, 1941, London, 1942. It was published in Pelican Books in 1945, in which form it became even more widely known.
[2] See P. Sargent Florence, *Ownership, Control and Success of Large Companies*. Sweet and Maxwell, London, 1961.
[3] John Day, New York, 1943.

term 'Machiavellian' to other works of political theory. As Sidney Anglo has recently pointed out, no other author has given rise to more English words than has Machiavelli – from 'Machiavellian to 'Machiavellize'.[1]

The interpretations of Machiavelli are legion. According to many commentators Machiavellian doctrine consisted in the advocacy of all that was most violent and devious in politics. From Machiavelli's own time onward he has been regarded as either diabolically inspired or at least as the teacher of evil. This interpretation stretches from Cardinal Pole through Frederick the Great's *Anti-Machiavel* to its most recent restatement by Professor Leo Strauss.[2] As Strauss says, this view has become unfashionable to the point of being ridiculed. Yet Strauss asks whether it is not strange *not* to call evil a man who appears to advocate the murder of political opponents, the imposition of severe instead of light penalties, or the confiscation of property.[3] To defend Machiavelli's doctrine as patriotic or as scientific is, for Strauss, merely to disguise the evil it teaches.

For other commentators, Machiavelli's supposed patriotism more than compensates for any necessary evils he may advocate. For still others, Rousseau being perhaps the most notable,[4] Machiavelli's notorious 'immorality' simply does not arise since *The Prince* is a satire on princes written by a convinced republican: 'He proposed to teach kings; but it was the people he really taught. His *Prince* is the book of Republicans.'

Still other commentators find the charge of immorality levelled against Machiavelli and 'Machiavellian' thinkers inappropriate for a different set of reasons. Following Croce, they claim that Machiavelli's greatness lay in his discovery of the 'autonomy of politics'.[5] Politics is for them an activity which obeys certain necessary laws which are, in their favoured phrase, 'beyond good and evil'. Their slogan might be 'politics is politics'. It is not a branch of morality but an activity which is concerned with, and is identifiable by its concern with, *raison d'état*. State necessity dictates all actions which are 'political' in any proper sense. According to Chabod, Machiavelli 'swept aside every criterion of action not suggested by the concept of *raison d'état*'.[6] Meinecke declared that the 'forceful political basis of truth in Machiavelli's *Principe*' lay in 'the

---

[1] S. Anglo, *Machiavelli: A Dissection* (Gollancz, London, 1969), p. 271.
[2] L. Strauss, *Thoughts on Machiavelli*, Free Press, Glencoe, Illinois, 1958. Reprinted University of Washington Press, Seattle, 1969.
[3] ibid., p. 9.
[4] *Social Contract* (Everyman edition, Dent, London, 1913), p. 59.
[5] F. Chabod, *Machiavelli and the Renaissance* (Bowes and Bowes, London, 1958), is a good instance of this genre. F. Meinecke, *Machiavellism* (Praeger, New York, 1965), reached similar conclusions by a different route.
[6] Chabod, p. 116.

discovery of the element of necessity in political conduct (and this is nothing else, succinctly expressed, than the essence of *raison d'état*)'.[1] Whatever the interest of the state demands is required of the 'good' politician, that is, one who is strong and skilled, endowed with Machiavellian *virtú*.

It is not denied that a morality exists – for private life. It is not even claimed that there is a state morality which is 'higher' than that of private life, though this is a doctrine which seems seldom far away.[2] Following *raison d'état* does however involve moral dilemmas which, for the defenders of this form of Machiavellianism, are of the highest order. These occur where the politician has to choose between private morality and the necessities of political action, however violent and cruel they may seem from the standpoint of ordinary morality. In recognizing this agonizing choice Machiavelli deserved Meinecke's highest praise:

> ... ultimately he was even capable of rising to the highest ethical feeling which is possible for action prompted by *raison d'état*; this sacrifice consists in taking on oneself personal disgrace and shame, if only it offers a means of saving the Fatherland.[3]

A Machiavellian then was, on this account, a man who coolly recognized the necessities of politics, who studied the 'State's first Law of Motion' and did so unimpeded by the irrelevancies of private morality.

Others, too, see in Machiavelli and Machiavellianism the source of the scientific study of politics and of its laws of motion without necessarily committing themselves to the thesis of the 'autonomy of politics'. Once more Machiavelli is ethically neutral, but this time it is the neutrality of the objective, 'value-free' political scientist of whom Machiavelli is sometimes said to be the first exemplar. Pollock claimed that

> The modern study of politics ... begins with Machiavelli ... we find in him, for the first time since Aristotle, the pure passionless curiosity of the man of science.[4]

Machiavelli, the political scientist, is portrayed as seeking to discern the underlying laws governing political relationships. The notorious 'problem' of the relation between *The Prince* and the *Discourses* is resolved by arguing that Machiavelli's aims and method remain constant but that his subject matter differs, the laws of principalities being different from those governing republican politics. Such

[1] Meinecke, p. 294.
[2] See Meinecke's struggle with this question throughout *Machiavellism*, but in particular in the opening and final chapters.
[3] ibid., p. 44.
[4] F. Pollock, *The History of the Science of Politics* (Macmillan, London, 1890; reprinted Beacon Press, Boston, 1960), p. 43.

interpretations take their inspiration from Machiavelli's own claims to have set the study of politics off in a new direction. The most celebrated statement is that in Chapter Fifteen of *The Prince* where he declares that he will

> ... depart from the methods of other people. But it being my intention to write a thing which shall be useful to him who apprehends it, it appears to me more appropriate to follow up the real truth of a matter than the imagination of it.[1]

Finally, there is the version of Machiavellianism which sees it as the scientific study of politics in a practical rather than an academic sense. Machiavelli's science is the science of statecraft:

> We must not say ... that he took hold of political theory and transported it from speculative realms to a region of empirical observation. The subject of his labour was the science of statecraft, and ... he made this science more theoretical than before.[2]

Machiavelli still embarks on a new way in political theory which involves ignoring traditional ethical concerns of philosophers such as Plato or the authors of the mirrors for princes. But now Machiavelli is portrayed as transforming the findings of Renaissance diplomacy into a theoretical science. It is however a 'policy science' specifically oriented to political practice, however neutral in its language. Basing, or allegedly basing himself, on scientific findings the Machiavellian advises his patient or his client, whether prince or republican, what it is in his interests to do: 'if you are a prince/republican and *if* you wish to achieve end *x*, *then* you must follow policy *y*'. The objectives themselves are set by the political actors, not by the scientist of statecraft. Ethical neutrality is still preserved.

James Burnham had, then, a variety of 'Machiavellianisms' to draw upon, and the persuasiveness of his argument arises, to a considerable extent, from the skill with which he wove together many of these strains of thinking. Burnham's Machiavellians were a group of political sociologists writing at the end of the nineteenth and in the first decades of the twentieth centuries. Mosca, Michels and Pareto were the leading figures, and Sorel shared a number of intellectual attributes with them.

The leading characteristic of Burnham's Machiavellianism is that it is an 'objective science of politics, comparable in its methods to the other empirical sciences'.[3] Machiavelli's method itself is described as the

---

[1] *The Prince*, Evergreen edition (Dent, London, 1952), p. 83.
[2] H. Butterfield, *The Statecraft of Machiavelli* (Bell, London, 1955), p. 22.
[3] *The Machiavellians*, p. 251 ff.

'method of science applied to politics'.[1] This scientific method consists in firstly describing and accumulating facts which may be drawn from direct observation or from political literature – in particular the works of history. Secondly, on the basis of these facts hypotheses are formulated. Thirdly, scientific method is morally and politically neutral in that it proceeds by testing these hypotheses by publicly available facts. Science cannot be politically committed.

Machiavellianism regards politics as the struggle for power. Hence political science is a science of power. It is an overt and essential principle of the science that it reduces all conflict to power terms. Public interest, welfare, justice are not, on this view, scientific terms but part of the ideology which supports the structure of power. A Machiavellian does not take such ideologies or myths to be 'true' or 'false' since those are irrelevant categories. He will, however, examine to what use ideology is put in the political power struggle – this is a matter of ascertainable fact.

Machiavellians, in Burnham's view, will not take as a basis of their science the theories of political philosophers or the programmes of political parties, but will seek the truth behind the illusion. When a politician speaks of the general welfare, the appropriate Machiavellian response would be to examine the policy to see which party in the power struggle stands to benefit from the proposal. In this respect Machiavellianism is comparable to the interest or group theory of politics associated with Bentley and Truman, which has exercised enormous influence on modern political science over the last twenty-five years.[2] But to the extent that interest theory takes as a working assumption that interest groups act rationally and logically in pursuit of their goals, Machiavellianism parts from it. Despite seeing politics as the pursuit of power, Machiavellians do not consider most political action to be deliberately conceived and logically carried through. Rather the contrary – most political conduct stems from instinct or emotion and its outcome is often far from what was intended by the political actors.

The struggle for power is between élite and non-élite or counter-élite. It follows that political science takes as its subject matter the composition of the élite, the formulation of its policy, its strategy and its relationship to the non-élite. Each élite seeks to promote its own interests although, because of the non-logical mode of its conduct, it is frequently less than successful. It promotes its interests by 'force and fraud' – always essential words in any Machiavellian vocabulary. Force may be actual or threatened, institutionalized and authoritative or

[1] ibid., p. 45.
[2] A. F. Bentley, *The Process of Government*. Principia Press, Bloomington, 1949; D. Truman, *The Governmental Process*. Knopf, New York, 1951.

revolutionary. Fraud is essentially enshrined in the ideology of an élite or of a particular era and the mode of relations between élite and non-élite.

The study of élites is not static but dynamic since the power-struggle is ceaseless. Élites give way to new élites – history is the 'graveyard of aristocracies'. No élite has ever been found capable of stemming the tide of history; there can be no millennium when the struggle will cease and politics will cease. Neither can there be a classless egalitarian society. Politics and power are part of the human condition and it is the laws of this part of man's estate that Machiavellianism aims to uncover. To be effectively scientific, politics must resolve the study of institutions into the élites which establish them, run them and transform them. Similarly the study of 'great men' or 'world-historical figures' must see such men in relation to the élites which they represent and which granted them support. 'When the élites are stated, everything is stated.'

It is possible to discern two major claims made by and on behalf of this Machiavellian style of politics. The first is that, as a method, it offers a true science of politics. The second is that it provides a 'brutally realistic' account of the craft of politics. Both claims are made on behalf of Machiavelli at least by Burnham. The Machiavellians' own attitude to Machiavelli is somewhat more ambivalent. Pareto shows considerable enthusiasm for his alleged intellectual forbear: 'Machiavelli, who "like an angel soareth" over the multitude of ethical historians.'[1] Pareto praises Machiavelli in precisely Burnham's terms. Machiavelli sought in scientific manner the uniformities of political history. He was falsely or, indeed, irrelevantly accused of immorality, whereas the only appropriate response should have been to examine the truth or falsity of his conclusions. He did not teach princes to be tyrants, but examined the workings of princely politics in *The Prince* and republican politics in *The Discourses*, and in the course of both demonstrated the realities of power relations – how to attain power, how to maintain it and how to lose it. Only the imperfect state of knowledge prevented him, like his one great predecessor Aristotle, from developing a sociology of politics in the modern manner.[2]

Mosca's attitude was much cooler. He acknowledges that Machiavelli had considerable aptitude for political science and, like Pareto, points to the imperfection of historical knowledge at Machiavelli's time.[3] Mosca is, however, much more insistent on Machiavelli's shortcomings as a political observer, and in *The Ruling Class* he is critical of what

[1] V. Pareto, *The Mind and Society*, ed. Livingston (Jonathan Cape, London, 1935), §2532.
[2] ibid., §1975.
[3] G. Mosca, *Histoire des doctrines politiques* (Pargot, Paris, 1936), pp. 116 ff.

Butterfield was later to describe as Machiavelli's abstract 'Machiavellism of the study'. *The Prince*, Mosca affirms, has 'been too much reviled and too much praised. In any event, whether in praise or in blame, too great an importance has been attached to it'.[1] Moreover, Machiavelli was, Mosca argues on the first page of *The Ruling Class*, less concerned with determining constant trends in history than in studying the practical arts of power.

The criterion by which both Mosca and Pareto tested Machiavelli's achievement as a political scientist was his success in discerning constant patterns in history. This is highly indicative of the character of Machiavellian political science. Its object is to discover general laws in politics.[2] Its data are the findings of history which can and do reveal such constancies. The uniformity of nature and of history is a basic assumption of Machiavellian political science. Without this assumption it would be correspondingly more difficult to develop laws which were generally applicable to all forms of political life throughout history – which is the stated objective of Machiavellianism.

This is certainly also the working assumption of Machiavelli's political thought. Nature, including political nature, is uniform. Consequently historical situations recur in a sufficiently similar manner for students of history to be able to draw political lessons for present-day politics. To deny this, Machiavelli says, is to speak

> ... as if the stars, the sun, the elements, and man, had in their motion, their order, and their capacity, become different from what they used to be.[3]

This is not to say that there is no change in history, but that this change occurs in an ascertainable manner. In common with other writers of his period and up to the eighteenth century, Machiavelli held that this change was a cyclical one, in which good political constitutions degenerated into bad and were ultimately renovated, only to be once more corrupted.

The discovery of such patterns constituted Machiavelli's 'new method' and what subsequent commentators have wished to describe as his new political science. It could also be the basis of an 'applied science' of statecraft where a political actor learned to imitate those

---

[1] *The Ruling Class* (McGraw-Hill, New York, 1939), Chapter VIII, §1, pp. 202–3.

[2] Pareto, 'The quest for uniformities is an end in itself', *The Mind and Society*, §2411.

[3] Machiavelli, *Discourses*, ed. L. J. Walker (Routledge and Kegan Paul, London, 1950), Book I, Preface, p. 206.

actions in history which had brought success either in gaining new glory or in postponing the inevitable degeneration. Given that political nature was constant, it was possible to assume that men had always been moved in history by like passions and interests: 'in all peoples there are the same desires and the same inclinations as there always were. So that if one examines with diligence the past, it is easy to foresee the future of any commonwealth.'[1] Like causes give rise to like effects. Hence it is possible to draw historical generalizations which serve as a 'scientific' basis for 'maxims' of statecraft. If history shows that only armed prophets conquer, then the appropriate political maxims for both nervous rulers and ambitious prophets are readily apparent.

This assumption of the uniformity of human nature was made by political thinkers and historians up to the late eighteenth century. David Hume believed that if one wished to understand the ancient Greeks and Romans one should study the character and motivations of the modern French and English. The assumption was revived by the modern Machiavellians. Mosca claims:

> Anyone who has travelled a good deal ordinarily comes to the conclusion that underneath superficial differences in customs and habits human beings are psychologically very much alike the world over; and anyone who has read history at all deeply reaches a similar conclusion with regard to the various periods of human civilization. Dipping into the documents that tell us how people of other ages felt, thought and lived, we come always to the same conclusion: that they were very much like us.[2]

Similarly Pareto believed that human nature had changed very little throughout Western history.[3] He assumes that there exist certain human instincts or states of mind which have remained virtually constant. These instincts or states of mind are not themselves the subject matter of social science. Their existence is revealed in the course of human theorizing which, Pareto claims, displays certain constant elements termed 'residues' which are the manifestations of the underlying psychic states. These 'residues' change very little and, being overt, can be studied by the sociologist. Their constancy permits them to be classified, and Pareto finds that two classes in particular are socially and politically significant. 'Class I' residues reflect the propensity to put together ideas, to innovate, to change. 'Class II' residues reflect the instinct to

---

[1] *Discourses*, I, 39, 1, p. 302.
[2] *The Ruling Class*, Chapter I, §16, p. 39.
[3] cf. §2450, 'If, for instance, one would clearly understand what happened in ancient Athens, one must consider what happened in France beginning with the ministry of Waldeck-Rousseau.'

consolidate, to conserve, to integrate. Adopting Machiavelli's terms the 'foxes' are those who use their imagination, the 'lions' are those who conserve.

As with Machiavelli, the constancy of human nature does not imply for these Machiavellians that history does not change. Politics is the sphere of the struggle for social power, and the Machiavellians hold that this struggle continues between élites. Their explanations of the causes of political change do differ to some extent.[1] Mosca and Michels find that élites rise and fall from a combination of organizational and personal factors. Minorities by force and cunning exploit their organizational advantages over minorities, but in turn they cannot afford to become too alienated from the society they endeavour to control. The ability to exploit a situation is related to the ability to understand it and this is recognizable by the élite's readiness to incorporate or make concessions to the various social groups in the society as a whole. To the extent that the élite does open its ranks to new blood it changes in character. If it fails to do so it becomes stultified, alienated from the society and open to revolutionary overthrow.

Pareto's account of social change is in terms of the changing *distribution* of Class I and Class II residues in the élite. This distribution can change comparatively rapidly as élites of 'lions' forcibly displace élites of 'foxes' who ultimately return to power by infiltrating the 'lion' élite. Neither the 'fox' style nor the 'lion' style of politics is ever in itself capable of holding on to power. 'Foxes' lack the propensity to use violence in defence of their power-position: 'lions' lack the cunning and imagination to respond to the inevitable flux of social and political life. But it is a central tenet of Machiavellianism that *both* force and fraud are essential if power is to be obtained and to be maintained.

The Machiavellians, relying on their assumptions about the uniformity of nature, turn to history to adduce a mass of supportive evidence for their hypotheses on the nature of political power. If Mosca's reading is extensive, Pareto's is truly staggering. In defending a thesis on the recurrent character of bureaucracy Mosca called in evidence Egypt, China, Rome and Napoleonic France. Pareto discovered examples of the cunning rule of 'Class I' élites in fifth- and fourth-century Athens,[2] late Republican Rome,[3] Renaissance Italy,[4] Louis Bonaparte's France[5] and Lloyd George's Britain where the government of England

---

[1] See further G. Parry, *Political Elites* (Allen and Unwin, London, 1969), Chapter II.
[2] *The Mind and Society*, §§2343–57.
[3] ibid., §2548.
[4] ibid., §§2529–37.
[5] ibid., §§2462–66.

had fallen into the hands of Welsh and Irish fanatics.¹ The Machiavellians naturally regarded this evidence as conclusive verifications of their various analyses of political power. In Burnham's view the Machiavellians were 'the only ones who have told us the full truth about power'.² A closer analysis of their historical science may, however, give rise to some doubt on this issue.

The Machiavellian approach to history would be better described as 'pre-historic'. In many respects the writing of history in a modern sense may be dated from the late eighteenth century, when writers began to abandon the Machiavellian practice of treating history as a 'storehouse of precedents' or as 'philosophy teaching by examples' and instead attempted by a process of empathy to understand the past on its own terms.³ They came to see the task of historical science as the recreation from existing records of a particular past way of life. Their stress lay on the 'individuality' and 'uniqueness' of the past. Historical nature was not constant. To understand the interests and motives of past actors required an effort of imagination comparable to the imaginative leap an anthropologist might have to make in order to understand the complex customs of a tribal society. The past had to be thought of as 'strange'. It would not be understood simply by understanding the modern English and French. This view of history, often associated with Collingwood,⁴ has recently been extended and adapted by Peter Winch to a view of the methods of social science as a whole.⁵ Winch treats social conduct as essentially 'rule-following', and argues that any 'scientific' account of it must be in terms of the rules and concepts of the society or the activity under investigation. The categories used to describe a religious rite or a political conflict must be appropriate to these sorts of activities in the particular society. Sociology is hence culture-bound.

Clearly, the Machiavellian approach to history runs totally contrary to this way of thinking and, indeed, Winch takes Pareto to be a prime example of the approach to sociology which he wishes to counter.⁶ While it must be acknowledged that difficulties arise with both Collingwood's account of history and with Winch's idea of a social science,⁷

[1] ibid., §244.
[2] *The Machiavellians*, p. 277.
[3] See F. Meinecke, *Die Entstehung des Historismus*. Munich and Berlin, 1936.
[4] R. G. Collingwood, *The Idea of History*. Oxford U.P., Oxford, 1946.
[5] P. Winch, *The Idea of a Social Science*. Routledge and Kegan Paul, London, 1958.
[6] *The Idea of a Social Science*, pp. 95–111.
[7] Extensive literatures exist on both. As an introduction to the historical problems see W. Dray, *Laws and Explanation in History*. Oxford U.P., London, 1957. On Winch see the recent discussion and the further references in Alan Ryan, *The Philosophy of the Social Sciences*. Macmillan, London, 1970.

the Machiavellian approach is undoubtedly damaged by this criticism. Machiavellian political generalizations are constructed by abstracting particular aspects of past conduct or past theory from their historical and social contexts and aggregating them. Mosca was unconsciously revealing of the Machiavellian method when he spoke of the student 'dipping into the records of history' since 'dipping' is precisely the term to describe their method. Mosca and Pareto 'dipped' into history to discover conduct which would verify their hypotheses about the rise and fall of élites or the frequency of non-logical behaviour. But the most persistent 'dipping' does not add up to a science and, as Sir Karl Popper has reminded us, it is the easiest thing in the world to accumulate 'verifications'.

The Machiavellian method of aggregating historical instances into a composite picture of political activity is fallacious. It results in the attribution to persons and groups of potential and actual powers possessed by allegedly similar persons and groups in the past. This is then presented as a composite account of the political power possessed by all present and future groups. The logical leap is obvious yet Mosca, in particular, employs it regularly in his account of the advantages possessed, in principle, by minorities as compared with majorities. Power can only be understood contextually. There is then some possibility of assessing whether any group has the kind of power appropriate to the situation. It is, however, this context which is lacking in Machiavellian analysis.

Pareto's division of theory into the constant element, 'residue' and the variable element 'derivation' is a further instance of the fallacy. 'Derivations' are what other writers have termed 'ideologies'. Pareto claims that 'derivations' merely provide a veneer of logic which masks the constant residues, which in turn manifest the constant state of mind. Thus the residues have been decked out by any number of 'derivations' in the course of human history which seek to rationalize what is fundamentally instinctual. The theologies and philosophies of the Moslem, the Catholic, the Calvinist, the Kantian and the Hegelian give very different explanations why one should not steal.[1] This, for Pareto, indicates that they are all rationalizations of a common residue. Marxism, similarly, has in common with Christianity the fact that it is a mere derivation.

This permits Pareto to indulge in a sustained satire on religious and on political and moral philosophies both celebrated and obscure. The satire is often acute, the cross-cultural comparisons are frequently amusing and indeed important. All are reduced to rationalizations usually of some power advantage accruing to an interested party – though that

[1] *The Mind and Society*, §1416.

party is not necessarily aware of the nature of the rationalization and may, as much as anyone, be victim of the illusion. But Pareto throws the baby out with the bath-water. He fails to perceive the interpenetration of ideas and context and consequently cannot allow for the individuality of societies and of historical epochs. Theories cannot be adequately described by reducing them to a constant and a variable element, by extracting the constant and making it represent the real force in history. To say that the 'divine right' theory of the seventeenth century and the twentieth-century theory of universal suffrage are equivalent because they are both legitimizing derivatives is to omit too much that is historically and sociologically significant. The kind of regime legitimized and the form of legitimation which can convince are interrelated in a way which Machiavellian reductionism cannot explain.

As Winch argues, the Christian would be correct in protesting against Pareto that Christian baptismal rites are not the same, or even virtually the same, as apparently similar pagan rites. This is not to say that the Christian theology is true – which is one of the dangers Pareto and Machiavellians wish to guard against in their sociology. But it is to say that what Pareto calls the 'derivation' is essential to the very understanding of what he calls the 'residue'. If this is so, then the existence of residues themselves must be in doubt. Pareto's own proof of them is highly unsatisfactory. As S. E. Finer has pointed out,[1] Pareto takes the acts which are supposed to manifest the residues to be evidence of the existence of the residues themselves. But even if residues or constant sentiments existed, it would not by itself follow that they would be of great significance in sociological or historical explanation. To say that men are always motivated by interest or by fear is by itself uniformative. What is significant is *what* is seen to be in one's interest in a particular era, or *what* it is that people fear – excommunication, inflation, creeping socialism. By dismissing these differentiating factors as insignificant Pareto is, as Winch says

... Inadvertently removing from his subject-matter precisely that which gives them sociological interest; namely their internal connection with a way of living.[2]

The Machiavellian approach permits cross-cultural comparisons of often startling originality but it fails, not from the capacity of its practitioners but as a result of its very methodology, to explain historical

---

[1] See the critique in his Introduction to *Vilfredo Pareto, Sociological Writings* (Pall Mall, London, 1966), p. 72 ff.
[2] *The Idea of a Social Science*, pp. 108–9. For a defence of Pareto against Winch see A. J. Baker, 'The Philosophical "Refutation" of Pareto', *Mind*, LXIX, 1960, pp. 234–43.

and social differentiation and the process of change. Reducing the science of politics to a science of force and fraud, Machiavellianism fails to give an adequate account of either because it fails to appreciate the conceptual relationship between mind and society which it is the Machiavellians' object to elucidate.

These considerations may also throw doubt upon the scientific basis of Machiavellian statecraft. Their quest was for uniformities but, as with Machiavelli himself, the supposed timeless quality of their generalizations about the nature of power can easily be read as timeless precepts concerning its use. If the Machiavellians are, as they claim, successful in explaining historically the operations of politics in terms of power, and if history repeats itself in its essential features, then the political inferences for a 'new prince' seem clear.

Did the Machiavellians have a 'new prince' in mind? Who constituted the audience for their new political science? Burnham's reply is that the Machiavellian science is entirely neutral. Traditional political thought – he takes Dante as his example – was merely a disguised form of propaganda. Machiavellian thought is concerned with truth; it contains no hidden meanings. Mosca, Burnham states, in expounding the theory of the ruling class, is not making a moral judgement.[1] Machiavellians, he argues in connection with Michels, do not assume the desirability of democracy or justice or any other ideal goal.[2] Pareto, he affirms, does not express any social or governmental ideal.[3] Burnham makes similar claims on his own behalf in *The Managerial Revolution*.[4]

There is a weak but significant sense in which even the most 'value-free' social and political theory, such as Burnham's, cannot remain neutral and that is in its effect. The use to which an empirical political theory may be put is no part of the theory itself, but is undoubtedly politically significant, especially when the theory purports to give some real insight into the politician's craft. In this sense explanation and injunction are inseparable. Any analysis of a political concept, such as 'power' or even 'politics', is intended to recommend itself to the readership, which may include the political practitioner. As Raphael has pointed out, analysis clarifies and improves concepts and may not leave the concept with the meaning it originally had in common usage.[5]

The new way of thinking about politics can serve to organize further

[1] *The Machiavellians*, p. 105.
[2] ibid., p. 149.
[3] ibid., p. 191.
[4] See *The Managerial Revolution*, p. 7.
[5] D. D. Raphael, *Problems of Political Philosophy* (Pall Mall, London, 1970), Chapter 1. See also Hugh Stretton, *The Political Sciences* (Routledge and Kegan Paul, London, 1969), Chapter 13.

theories whether empirical or openly normative in intention. This is fully appreciated by Burnham:

And though this book contains no programme and no morality, if the theory which it puts forward is true, or partly true, no intelligent programme of social morality is possible without an understanding of this theory.[1]

It is this consideration which can justify critics down the ages in describing Machiavelli as a teacher of evil. Indifference to the effect of political theorizing is, for them, morally culpable.

The indispensable condition of 'scientific' analysis is then moral obtuseness.[2]

This consideration, too, has weighed with many of the commentators on Machiavellian political theory who have doubted the Machiavellians' neutrality or who have seen them as the witting or unwitting mentors of Fascism.[3]

Intellectually and politically Machiavellian thought was intended as a reply to Marxism. Just as Burnham's work has been described as a 'Marx for the managers',[4] so Burnham's Machiavellians may in many respects be regarded as providing a 'Marx for the bourgeoisie'. In replying to Marxism the Machiavellians were attempting to refute a science which was not merely explanatory but which had an overt practical intent. Marxism offered a scientific prediction that the bourgeois ruling class would be overthrown by a conscious proletariat, and an explanation of the revolutionary process which was also a guide to revolutionary action. Marxist science would itself assist the revolutionary consciousness and expedite the replacement of class rule by a classless society. The proletariat was thus armed by an ideology in the form of a science. Machiavellianism offered a scientific refutation of Marxism which could itself serve as an ideology or an organizing myth.

Machiavellianism aimed at dealing three blows to Marxist 'scientific socialism'. Firstly, it would show, on the basis of historical evidence, that Marxist predictions of a future classless society were without any empirical justification, that on the contrary élitism was inevitable. Secondly, it would display Marxism in its true non-scientific colours as a myth comparable to the influential religions of the past. Thirdly, it

[1] *The Managerial Revolution*, p. 8.
[2] Leo Strauss, *Thoughts on Machiavelli*, p. 11.
[3] On Pareto in this connection see S. E. Finer's penetrating assessment in 'Pareto and Pluto-Democracy: The Retreat to Galapagos', *American Political Science Review*, LXII, No. 2, June 1968.
[4] H. H. Gerth and C. W. Mills, 'A Marx for the Managers', *Ethics*, LII, 1941–42, pp. 200–215.

would, in demonstrating the inevitability of élite rule, describe the techniques of political power – the rules of the craft of politics.

These rules, though in the proper scientific spirit made available to the political public at large, nevertheless might be expected to give particular encouragement to the hard-pressed bourgeoisie. Not only was their extermination not inevitable, they were especially well-fitted to survive. The Machiavellians described what was necessary organizationally and personally if power was to be achieved and maintained. Organizational forces in particular favoured the bourgeoisie. Mosca and Michels argued for the inherent advantages of minority organization over the mere weight of numbers. Such organized minorities would be self-conscious, self-confident, able to act and react swiftly as a result of their cohesiveness. But such organization required skill – in obtaining information, in communicating, in theorizing, in financing. These skills are bureaucratized and hence become routines which are all the more difficult to dislodge. The practitioners come to possess what Mosca usefully termed the advantages of *positions déjà prises*. The skills involved were those already possessed by the middle class. They were skills which required education and experience or bureaucratic or managerial training which were already the perquisities of the bourgeoisie. Anyone who aspired to such élite positions would need to acquire these skills and would became 'bourgeoisified'. He would be assimilated into the middle class. Organization, however, was insufficient without ruler-temperament and this, too, appeared to most Machiavellians to be a quality of the bourgeois or the bourgeoisified. Mosca in particular looked to the middle class to develop the political qualities which would safeguard civilization. Pareto alone stood apart. The most wide-ranging and systematic of the anti-Marxists amongst the Machiavellians, he nevertheless held no illusions, by the time of writing *The Mind and Society*, about the ruler-temperament of the contemporary bourgeoisie.[1]

The lack of such ruler-qualities is all the more important for Pareto in that he placed more stress on the psychology of ruling than did the other Machiavellians. In general outline they would all agree with Pareto on the necessary personal ingredients for the exercise of power, but he was, in this respect, undoubtedly the most 'Machiavelli-like' of all the Machiavellians. So Machiavelli-like was he that Machiavelli's two categories of ruler-types – 'lions' and 'foxes' – have come to be

---

[1] See again Finer's 'Pareto and Pluto-Democracy: The Retreat to Galapagos', *American Political Science Review*, LXII, No. 2, 1968, pp. 440–50, where this point is vigorously and brilliantly argued. In the very timely attempt to counterbalance the received opinion on Pareto, it seems to me that Professor Finer perhaps underplays the element of violence in *The Mind and Society*.

widely applied, and without too much distortion, to Pareto's own categories. This is a usage supported by Pareto's own practice, although he did not use the terms 'foxes' and 'lions' with any great frequency.

In common with all Machiavellians Pareto insisted again and again that governing involved the use of both force and fraud. 'Consent and force appear in all the course of history as instruments of governing.'[1] For Pareto, as for Machiavelli, a combination of the qualities of lion and fox would be that best equipped for political survival.[2] Such a mixture was, however, very rare and was, like all élites, unstable. The circulation of élites was attributable to the inelectable failure of élites to recognize the dual character of political power.

'Foxes' typically attempted to govern by 'consent', 'lions' to govern by 'force'. By consent was not meant 'the fiction of "popular representation" – poppycock grinds no flour'.[3] The rule of 'King Demos' was always illusory. An élite governed by consent when it was cunning enough to exploit the residues of the mass. It deceived the subject class into following a policy, supported by an ideology, which was beneficial to the power position of the foxes and which might, incidentally, be in the interest of the subjects as well. 'Consent', for Pareto, amounted to what a modern sociologist would term 'legitimation', and could extend to any process by which the subject population was persuaded to accept and 'internalize' the rules by which they were governed. A major test of statecraft was the skill with which the sentiments of the population were utilized to obtain consent.[4]

It was, however, scientifically mistaken and politically disastrous to suppose that this could be the only test. This was the trap that élites of 'foxes' fell into. They supposed that they could always discover some further stratagem, some further ideological trick, some further bribe which would maintain them in power. They were inherently incapable of employing the one instrument of governing which would sustain their position in the face of a counter-élite which had become resentful of being exploited and contemptuous of their mode of ruling. The 'foxes' were misled by inappropriate humanitarianism. They could not turn into 'lions' and hence would be swept away by lions capable of the necessary violence. Their humanitarianism led them to accept any excuse not to punish severely threats to their regime.

This, Pareto asserted, was the manner of the democracies of his day. The police were criticized for acting 'impulsively' if they protected themselves. Courts were accused of being too severe in their sentences or

[1] *The Mind and Society*, §2251.
[2] ibid., §2190.
[3] ibid., §2244.
[4] *The Mind and Society*, §2247.

of being instruments of class-dominance. Governments desisted from protecting employers against strikes when accused of interfering with free economic bargaining.[1] Expressions of pity for suffering increased regardless of whether the suffering was useful to the society. This was coupled with pacific ideologies.[2] Campaigns were mounted to abolish capital punishment.[3] These attitudes and their attendant derivations merely prepared the way for the élite's downfall. The speculators of Rome brought on the fall of the Republic. The eighteenth-century French humanitarians prepared the way for the reign of terror. The early nineteenth-century liberals laid the basis for the period of demagogic oppression which Pareto saw looming.

To use a more recent (but no more perceptive) zoological terminology, Pareto, like all Machiavellians, was a 'hawk'. Statecraft required that violence should be met with violence. The élite must be prepared to defend itself and the regime with the force with which it was endowed by virtue of being a government. Otherwise it would yield to an élite of 'lions' which would employ force. This was an inevitable part of the historical process. It is, however, difficult to escape the conclusion that Pareto believed that such a weak-kneed élite *ought* to give way. At times Pareto seems to exult in the contemplation of violence. He sees it as a timely cleansing operation, as a form of political hygiene.

If the governing élite in 1789 had been prepared to counter force with force, if Louis XVI had been ready to die 'weapon in hand like a man of sinew', they might have saved themselves. As the élite did not act, 'it was salutary that its rule should give way to rule by others'. Similarly,

> If the victims of the September massacres, their kinsmen and friends, had not ... been spineless humanitarians ... they would have annihilated their enemies instead of waiting to be annihilated themselves. It was a good thing that power should pass into the hands of people who showed that they had the faith and the resolve requisite for the use of force.[4]

The Albigensians were massacred, the Renaissance Italians conquered, the French defeated in 1870 because they had become too fox-like and enervated to save themselves.

Pareto saw only one possible virtue in humanitarianism – that it would hasten the process of degeneration and hence the replacement of an unfit political organism by a fitter.[5] His contempt for modern

---

[1] All these instances are given in §2187.
[2] *The Mind and Society*, §§1142–3.
[3] ibid., §2520.
[4] *The Mind and Society*, §2191.
[5] ibid., §2480.

democracies which he believed combined all the worst features of the foxes – humanitarianism, political chicanery, economic corruption – led him to applaud those 'lions', of any political persuasion, who refused to join the circus but instead sought a violent confrontation:

> ... the use of force is indispensable to society; and when the higher classes are averse to the use of force ... it becomes necessary, if society is to subsist and prosper, that that governing class be replaced by another which is willing and able to use force. Roman society was saved from ruin by the legions of Caesar and Octavius. So it may happen that our society will one day be saved from decadence by the heirs of the Syndicalists and Anarchists of our day.[1]

Governments which go half-way are doomed. As Machiavelli noted, if one is to be violent one must know how to go about it. In the conflict between the fox and the lion it is the lion which kills the fox in the end.[2] It is impossible not to detect the note of admiration which enters Pareto's language when he refers to the confrontation he believed and hoped would develop in Italy:

> So it is that the men who write for the *Avanti* [Mussolini was then editor] show that they have the qualities of virility and frankness, the qualities that assure victory in the end and which, after all, are beneficial to the nation as a whole. The fox may, by his cunning, escape for a certain length of time, but the day may come when the lion will reach him with a well-aimed cuff, and that will be the end of the argument.[3]

Machiavellian political science and Machiavellian statecraft are linked by their common denominator – power. As Burnham argued, Machiavellianism is fundamentally a science of power. This does not mean that it is a science of violence. Machiavellians repeatedly deny that any regime can govern solely by force. The violence that Pareto held to be essential to politics, and whose *discriminating* use he so much admired, was only one of the two instruments of governing. Any attempt to govern by force alone would quickly fail. Some form of consent was necessary, and it was the weakness of the 'lions' that they were insufficiently imaginative to exploit the sentiments of the subjects without assistance from the 'foxes'. Machiavellianism should not be thought of as the source of a theory of political violence but rather as one of the chief expositions, along with Marx, of the role of political ideology. Whether termed 'ideologies', 'derivations' or 'political formulae' they

[1] *The Mind and Society*, §1858.
[2] ibid., §2480 n. 4.
[3] *The Mind and Society*, §2480 n. 1.

play a crucial part in the Machiavellian explanation of political order and of disorder, of stability and of revolution, To say that the Machiavellians ignored the role of ideas in politics could scarcely be more mistaken.

Nevertheless Machiavellianism remains a theory of power if not of violence. The account of ideology and consent is itself entirely manipulative. Consent is gained by the manipulation of sentiments – a manipulation which need not be entirely conscious.[1] Moral and philosophical systems are all treated in a reductionist manner and interpreted as 'great superstitions' or 'universal illusions'. Political moralities are all more or less transparent rationalizations of sentiments or interests. This analysis of politics and morality undoubtedly has a cutting edge. As Finer points out, the effectiveness of Pareto in particular is undeniable. Yet such a conception of politics in terms of power has its inbuilt limitations.[2] Though the Machiavellians take account of ideas in politics and history they do not respect them. Despite their intentions they 'take the mind out of history'. Unable to recognize the contextual connection between ideas, sentiments and interests, they are methodologically unable to account for historical and social differentiation. Instead they are forced to regard historical events as curiosities which will serve to illustrate the universal laws of politics. They are able consequently to dismiss counter-examples as unimportant instead of investigating their character. Their history is as selective, if not more so, than their Marxist opponents.[3]

The Machiavellians thus combine reductionism and verificationism. Without any means of individuating political societies their understanding of politics is correspondingly diminished. In some ways they are like modern systems theorists who can display any and every society in systemic terms, pointing out political analogies hitherto overlooked, but who are methodologically crippled when attempting to characterize what distinguishes the politics of Britain from that of the Philippines. Like a recent British Prime Minister they may almost be accused of taking politics out of politics.

To claim that Machiavellianism is committed to undervaluing ideas is not to argue that political science should moralize in the manner which Pareto in particular so scathingly denounced. Nor is it merely to repeat the point that political science must recognize the normative character of any form of knowledge which aims at improving our understanding

[1] Mosca, *The Ruling Class* III, §1, p. 71.
[2] Apart, that is, from the obscurities of the notions of power involved. See G. Parry, *Political Elites*.
[3] See S. E. Finer's comments in the Introduction to *Vilfredo Pareto: Sociological Writings*, p. 77.

and which hence changes the world it describes. It is claimed, rather, that the nature of politics is insufficiently explained by Machiavellianism. It offers an explanation of how men participate politically but not why they participate. It is unable to comprehend a view of politics which holds that political action is of the utmost value because it will realize human potentialities. It is unable to comprehend a view which holds that politics is the arena in which the individual is to cultivate his capacity for responsibility and self-determination. It is not enough for a Machiavellian to reply that these are norms and not facts, and hence not his concern. To the extent that political behaviour and political institutions rest on such views and in turn promote then, they will not be fully understood by the Machiavellian or even taken seriously, but will be dismissed as the products of 'false consciousness'.

But lest they be so dismissed, it may be better to take a final example which should illustrate the Machiavellian inability to explain Machiavellian politics even on its own terms. From the first, rivalling the view of Machiavelli as the teacher of evil, has been the view that he was the teacher of liberty. True to *both* Machiavellian traditions the modern Machiavellians proclaim to a man their loyalty to this one ideal of liberty. They are, Burnham asserts,

> ... very profoundly concerned with the reality of democracy defined as liberty. They know that the degree of liberty present within a society is a fact of the greatest consequence for the character of the whole social structure and for the individuals living within that structure.[1]

The subtitle of *The Machiavellians* is 'Defenders of Freedom'.

'Only power restrains power'[2] summarizes one major theme of Machiavellian thinking. Liberty emerges from the conflict between élite and counter-élite or between the social forces which make up society. Mosca, Michels and Burnham all enunciate this in their concluding chapters. Democracy in any such sense as Rousseau's is said to be unrealizable, but the society as a whole benefits from the power conflict as the élite or their rivals are forced to make concessions in order to secure popular backing. For a country to be free, Mosca argues, power must curb power. Social forces must balance other social forces. The greatest danger to liberty occurs where political organization is organized so as to concentrate all power in one set of hands whether elected, appointed or merely usurped. The hope for liberty currently lies, in Mosca's view, in the mutual checks and balances between

[1] *The Machiavellians*, p. 275.
[2] ibid., p. 278.

bureaucracy and democracy.[1] The object of social policy must then be to maximize the opportunity for social forces to make their impact on government, and to act as mutual checks for the sake of liberty.[2]

This form of defence of liberty is certainly respectable and has a long heritage. The Machiavellians are, however, unable fully to participate in this heritage since they are unable to explain and defend the liberty they proclaim as an ideal. They point to the effects of such liberty in promoting scientific understanding, social mobility or 'civilization', but provide no reason why these ideals should not be dismissed as ideologies or rationalizations, along with the other creeds whose pretensions they claim so successfully to have demolished. Perhaps it is this inability to explain and justify their own ideals and consequently to comprehend the full spectrum of politics that explains the moral despair which continually appears in the midst of the Machiavellians' scientific optimism. They both relish the shock which good democrats and liberals will experience when confronted with their scientific findings, and at the same time express a certain regret that political life has to be as they find it.

> The democratic currents of history resemble successive waves. They break ever on the same shoal. They are ever renewed. This enduring spectacle is simultaneously encouraging and depressing.[3]

Not finding any viable justification for their ideals they, not surprisingly, were unable to discover any satisfactory institutional defence of them. Hence, perhaps, their political wanderings. Mosca began as an iconoclastic critic of representative democracy and ended reluctantly defending representative democracy and himself a representative.[4] Michels began as a socialist yet became disillusioned with the democratic pretensions of socialism, and ended his days sympathetic to Mussolini.[5] Pareto was at the outset a thorough-going radical liberal. By the end of his career he had become contemptuous of all existing political forms, and in particular a ferocious and bitter satirist of liberal democracy. He looked to a new force to cleanse the Italian stable, and seemed at moments to see some hope in Mussolini, who in turn honoured him. Yet it is clear that his own theory could give him no hope that such

---

[1] *The Ruling Class*, Chapter V, §§7–11, pp. 138–47.
[2] ibid., Chapter X, §6, p. 258. See also Burnham, *The Machiavellians*, pp. 275–93.
[3] Michels, *Political Parties*, p. 425.
[4] See J. Meisel's brilliant account of Mosca's intellectual career, *The Myth of the Ruling Class*. University of Michigan Press, Ann Arbor, 1958. Note Meisel's own chapter on Mosca's relation to Machiavelli.
[5] See R. Michels, *First Lectures in Political Sociology* (University of Minnesota Press, Minneapolis, 1949), esp. Chapter VI.

'lions' could better defend the ideals he espoused. So he retired to the life of a private scholar – 'the retreat to the Galapagos Islands'.

Professor Finer's comment on Pareto may serve for all the Machiavellians. He suggests that Pareto's rage and chagrin is that of the lover betrayed by his mistress.[1] And perhaps the Machiavellians were betrayed because they were unable to understand her.

[1] 'Pareto and Pluto-Democracy: The Retreat to Galapagos', loc. cit., p. 448.

Strikes, Trade Unions and the State

H. B. ACTON

I

The increase in the numbers of strikes and threats of strikes in democratic countries in recent years has led to a good deal of discussion about how to reduce their frequency, but rather less about the principles that ought to govern the relations between trade unions and the state. This is partly because employers and trade unions, industrial journalists and social theorists have prided themselves upon what they consider their realistic concern for the facts of life. The question, as they see it, is how the rest of the community can most effectively adjust to the activities of trade unions rather than the place that, rationally considered, trade unions should occupy in our society. Adjustment is a rather comfortable, conservative conception which, in the present context, might be used to suggest that Edmund Burke himself would have welcomed the Donovan Report and would have angrily consigned Mr Carr to the same class of legalistic nigglers as Charles Townshend and Lord North. On the other hand, even an opponent of Utopian abstractions may feel a little perturbed that writers on political philosophy have given so little attention to trade unions and to strikes.[1]

Earlier in the century when the views of Gierke and Maitland were under discussion, trade unions were considered among other social organizations that were thought to have and to deserve a life and scope free from domination by the state. The Taff Vale case and the Osborne decision gave rise to discussion of the function of trade unions and of the public interest by reference to them. Rookes versus Barnard,[2] on the other hand, although it occupied the courts for a long time, led to little public discussion of principles, partly, although by no means wholly,

---

[1] There is some discussion of the rights of unions in A. J. M. Milne's *Freedom and Rights* (London, 1968), Chapter 10.

[2] See, however, Douglas Rookes, *Conspiracy*. London, 1966.

because by this time the legal issues had become very complicated indeed. In the meantime, I need hardly say, trade unions had become very powerful.

It is worth noting, too, that one finds very little about strikes, their nature and purposes, in books of reference that might be expected to provide relevant information and analysis. There is little in the UNESCO *Dictionary of the Social Sciences* (London, 1964). John A. Fitch, the author of the article 'Strikes and Lockouts' in the *Encyclopaedia of the Social Sciences* (London, 1934) makes an interesting theoretical observation at the beginning of the article and concludes by saying that it is economic inequality 'which makes the strike inevitable', an obscure, and so far as the article goes, an unsupported judgement. But the ethics of the matter are hardly touched on. Nor are principles much considered in the article 'Labour Relations' in the *International Encyclopaedia of the Social Sciences* (New York, 1968). The author of this article points out that in totalitarian countries strikes are regarded as subversive, and goes on: 'Elsewhere strikes have outlived their criminal origins and have, in degree, become institutionalized as one of the acknowledged sanctions of collective bargaining.' My concern in this paper is to go beyond these matters of fact and law to consider some questions of nature and of right.

II

Let us first consider the question of nature or essence. A strike is the temporary refusal of an employee or of a group of employees to continue to work for their employer, with the object of obtaining for themselves an improvement in their terms of employment. Although a single employee with some monopoly skill might go on strike, it is with groups of employees that we are here concerned. The group that goes on strike might comprise all the employees of a given firm or all the employees of a certain grade or skill employed by that firm. These men might meet together to organize their strike without forming any continuing association, but nowadays strikes are undertaken, officially or unofficially, by employees as members of trade unions. Furthermore, as the principal trade unions are organized on the basis of the type of work done by the employee rather than on the basis of the employer they work for, strikes are often waged against all the employers in a given industry. Even before the coalmines and railways were nationalized, all the miners or all the railwaymen on occasion went on strike against all the mineowners or all the railway companies. It sometimes happens that only the members of one union go on strike but make it impossible for members of other unions to continue their work. The strike ends either with the employer agreeing to some or all or to some modification of the strikers' demands or with the strikers returning to work on the employer's terms. Nowadays defeated strikers generally expect to receive some 'face-saving' concession.

It will be noticed that I have defined a strike as 'a temporary refusal' to continue to work. The adjective 'temporary' was introduced to indicate that strikers intend to go on working for the same firm when the strike is over. The author of the article on strikes and lockouts in the *Encyclopedia of the Social Sciences* writes: 'Despite the legal contradictions involved, he [the striker] thinks of the job as his own to be claimed again w en the strike is settled. This point of view tends in part to explain the attitude of bitter hostility to strike breakers.' It is easy to imagine this happening when employees of a small firm strike against their employer in the absence of a trade union. In striking they would be trying to support or enforce their position in a temporary dispute between parties who are presumed to be in some continuous and perhaps long-term relationship. In a somewhat similar way, a woman could strike against her husband without contemplating divorce, and, just as the situation would have become very different if the husband invited another woman into the household, so the strike would cease to be a merely internal dispute between settled partners if the employer took on another set of employees.

When the strike is organized and conducted by a trade union, the reason why the strikers expect to return to their old jobs afterwards is rather different. If the strike is to succeed, most of the members must join it and non-members must be persuaded not to take their jobs. The employer is faced with the alternatives of agreeing to the union's terms or of being unable to produce the goods he is in business to sell. He would not be faced with this alternative and hence would not be under the same pressure to accept the union's terms, if he could employ other men at more advantageous terms to himself than the union is demanding for its members. This is the same thing as to say that the trade union limits or prevents competition between workmen for jobs. Members of the trade union try to prevent the employer from choosing other workmen to work for him more cheaply than they themselves are prepared to do. In limiting competition between workmen for jobs they limit the choice of workmen open to the employer in a somewhat similar way to that in which firms may agree among themselves not to sell their goods below a certain price. The striker does not want to compete with his fellows for jobs with firms, but is happy if firms compete among themselves to employ him.

It might seem to follow that trade unions are economic organizations comparable with firms and, in non-socialist societies, operating in markets. This, however, is not the case. Trade unions do not produce and sell products as firms do, although their activities affect the power of firms to do so. A firm might possibly be made more efficient by the necessity to meet the demands of a union, or it may be forced by the union to run at a loss or even to close down. But it is as workers that employees participate in industrial and commercial activities and as trade unionists that they influence results which they play no part in planning. The owner or the directors run the firm while the trade unions look after the interests of the employees while this is being done. The employer wants to make profits by selling goods, the employees to improve their position within the organization that has been set up to do this. Within this framework it is rational for employees and trade unions to want their firms and industries to make profits and to use their evidence of success as grounds for improvements in their wages and conditions. Within this framework, too, trade unions might be expected to advise their members to move away from unsuccessful firms to firms that can afford to pay them more.

III

But we all know that this is not how things are happening. From the welter and confusion of current events in industry we may select some circumstances of particular importance for the philosophy of society. Unions ask for wage increases from firms and industries which are in serious economic trouble.[1] This would be inexplicable if the union were thinking in terms of the framework mentioned above. Most trade unions in the United Kingdom, however, are affiliated to the Labour Party, which is in favour of 'public ownership' and officially opposed to the system of competitive capitalism. Almost all the officials of these trade unions and a large majority of their members share the Labour Party's attitude towards private industry, and some officials and members hold collectivist views of a more drastic character. Within the trade union movement, therefore, there is a widespread belief that employers are necessarily exploiters and that private industry is wicked.

For some, therefore, strikers are always on the side of good against evil, and for many more there is the idea that the bankruptcy of large firms would lead to their nationalization, and would hence promote the Labour Party's aims. Conservative governments, as much as Labour governments, they believe, would nationalize collapsing firms rather than allow the widespread unemployment that their closure would

---

[1] As this was being written it was reported that the National Union of Blast-furnacemen were to strike for a wage increase of 35 per cent. According to *The Times* leading article the British Steel Corporation, who were being asked to pay this, was 'an industry which has got into a financial and productive plight'.

bring about. Others are ready to go along with 'unofficial' Communist or Trotskyist leaders who put forward claims and call strikes which the recognized unions do not think timely or appropriate. Sometimes, indeed, the unions themselves call strikes in order to forestall the activities of these 'unofficial' leaders.[1] It is very seldom that union leaders are willing or able to expel from their unions the men who have instigated 'unofficial' strikes. Indeed, if such a strike is successful, it would appear that it ought to have been 'official', and it could be represented as absurd for the union to cashier the generals who had won the campaign just because their leadership was unconstitutional. 'Unofficial' strikes, therefore, are frequently 'recognized' by the 'official' trade union, and there are rational grounds for doing this within the ambit of the immediate interests of the strikers and the union.

On the other hand, employers must necessarily find such proceedings distasteful. For one thing, it must appear to them that the union is deceiving them when it claims to represent the men. For another, it seems unjust to the employers for the union to start by agreeing on certain terms with them and then to acquiesce in the 'unofficial' leaders' more onerous terms. The 'unofficial' leaders can be regarded as playing their part in an elaborate trick which the union leaders secretly welcome and publicly deplore. If the union leaders recognize in their negotiations that the firm is in a weak economic position, the more likely it is that they will be outflanked by the radicals.

Tactics of this sort may well have benefited the employees during periods of great industrial prosperity in the past. A reason for their continuing success has been the adoption by governments of Keynesian economic policies, which have made it possible for employers to recoup the apparently uneconomic wage settlements by charging higher prices for their products. The success of these 'full employment' policies has meant that the terms of bargaining have for many years favoured the employees. The employers, recognizing this, have decided they had better pay up and raise their prices rather than risk the losses that prolonged strikes would entail. With the advent of the Conservative Government of June 1970, however, a new general economic policy appears to have been attempted. Long and costly strikes have in some cases been followed by large wage increases, but unemployment has in

[1] According to *The Times*, this was the position in the Blastfurnacemen's strike mentioned on page 139. 'The Union's executive and general secretary are quick on the draw because they fear unofficial action, with the prospect of losing control of their members. That is just what happened two years ago at Port Talbot, and the difficulty there was in settling that dispute suggests that there is something to be said for an official – even if premature – strike if it forestalls a messy and protracted stoppage of the kind that occurred at Port Talbot.'

consequence increased and important firms have been forced into bankruptcy.

What the results are likely to be is not yet clear. What is clear is that Labour Party leaders oppose the policy of allowing large industrial firms to go bankrupt, and urge that they should be nationalized instead. Both union and 'unofficial' leaders support these ideas and continue to say that the Government should not and in fact will not allow the widespread unemployment that would result from the collapse of these firms. Increased unemployment has not so far prevented regularly repeated demands for large wage increases. There is indeed some doubt whether this unemployment has led to the expected improvement in the bargaining position of employers. But people are beginning to fear that uneconomic wage increases will prevent firms from obtaining the new capital they need. If this were to happen, capitalism would collapse, not as Marx prophesied, as a result of cut-throat competition between firms each seeking monopoly for itself, but as a result of wage settlements which make voluntary investment in industry unattractive. Instead of killing itself in the industrial carnage written of by Marx, capitalism would expire with the whimper of starved exhaustion.

IV

Let us now consider employers and trade unions strictly within the context of economic institutions and operations. The employer, in order to be able to sell goods at a profit, employs men to do the detailed work of producing them, and these men belong to a trade union which negotiates terms and conditions on their behalf. There is bargaining between the employer and the employees about terms and conditions of work, but it should be noticed that it is the employer who plans the sequence of operations, and if he had not seen prospects for profit, this particular enterprise would never have existed. Until well on in the present century employers in this country have been called 'masters', and employers in France are still called *patrons*. But from a purely economic point of view, an employer is a man or firm that pays workers for the work they do on his behalf. Masters are supposed to have authority over their servants, and until the seventies of the last century employees and their unions were legally regarded in that light. From a strictly economic point of view, however, a servant's obedience is paid for by the 'master' as part of the work that is done in exchange for money.

The authority of an employer, then, from the economic (and legal) point of view, is not the same as that of a head of a family. The employees are not children or servants or serfs. Yet on the other hand the relationship is not quite the same as that between the buyers and sellers of goods, where each party has rights and duties but neither is in authority over the other. For the employer does seem to have an authority which the employee does not have. It would seem that the employer is entitled to have the employee's obedience, whereas we do not say that the employer ought to obey the employees. On what does this apparent right of the employer to obedience from his employees depend, and how far does it extend?

I suggest the following answer to the first part of the question. Under a system of private enterprise it is the employer who has decided what it is he wants to make and sell, and who, therefore, has devised the general means for doing this. He cannot proceed without employees and he tells them what he needs to have done and what types of craftsmen he wants to employ. Those who respond enter the employer's organization to participate in the work that he has planned. He will see to it that the employees are told what to do. Part of this process of telling them what to do will consist in issuing orders about times of starting and ending work, of the types and amounts of work to be done between these times, the treatment to be given to the firm's raw materials and other property, and so on. All this involves rules and orders on the one side, and obedience on the other. We may see in this a disciplinary authority, as we may call it, involved in the methods by which the employer makes sure that the work he is paying for is being done. As initiator and organizer of the concern, the employer may be said to have authority in these respects as well, that is, the right to receive obedience from the employees who have chosen to work for him. He and his agents also give instructions to the employees in the details of their work.

Trained and skilled workers do not need much detailed instruction from above, and obedience is hardly called for here and, if enforced, may on occasion be to the detriment of the firm. 'Paint this dark green' is an order of the sort that is frequently necessary, but if the painter knows that the thing to be painted has to be visible in dim light, immediate obedience is hardly what is called for. Disciplinary and initiatory authority are not relevant to questions about how things are likely to turn out, or about what causes what. Here the employee may have much to tell the employer, and the employer might be wise to pay him for doing so.

The employees do not own the firm, have not founded it, and have not settled its organization and policies. They do not possess, therefore, the disciplinary and initiatory authority that flow from these things and belong to the employer. We must ask, however, whether employees do not have that aspect of disciplinary authority which is the right to exercise such supervision as will ensure that they get what they have contracted for. In an important respect, however, employers and employees are in very different positions even in this regard. The employer is buying work for which he gives money, and it is more difficult for him and needs much more arrangement, to ascertain that the right work is being done, than for the employee to ascertain that he has received the right money. The former is always a continuous process, the latter is generally a fairly easily completed act. (Payments that need very elaborate calculation can alter the situation.) Even so, if the employer is entitled to see that the work to be paid for is being done, the employees are entitled to see that they are not being made to do work for which they do not receive payment. I suggest that the outcome of this discussion is that whereas the disciplinary (or supervisory) authority of the employer merges with his initiatory and proprietory authority, the employees' disciplinary (supervisory) authority has nothing comparable to merge with. Indeed, 'authority' is hardly the correct word for the employees' right to *refuse* obedience, for authority is the right to *receive* it. Shop stewards are more like tribunes than consuls.

When in the first paragraph of this section I said that a master buys the obedience of his servant, I was stating the matter too vaguely. What the master or employer buys are services, the carrying out of which requires the employee to obey in certain matters. An employer's authority is his right to obedience from the employee. He is entitled to the obedience because it is an essential feature of the work or service he has bought. To buy obedience *tout court* would be to buy the man for the period for which the obedience was bought, and this would be slavery, even if only temporary.

Although it is economically reasonable for trade unions to bargain with employers over wages and conditions of work, this bargaining is very different from that between firms and customers or between one firm and another. Trade unions are not sellers of labour, since it is the individual workman who owns it, nor do trade unions produce goods as firms do. They are, in a sense, parasitic on firms, and may be regarded as making the production of their goods more difficult. If, as now often happens, employers' associations bargain with unions, the organs of industry are multiplied, extra wheels are added to the coach. G. D. H. Cole, writing in 1920, said that with the coming of trade unions and employers' associations 'almost all the economic forms of association are doubled', and the result of this duplication 'is not merely wasteful, but actively pernicious'.[1]

The trade union's function of making the best possible bargain on behalf of its members is not necessarily consistent with the interests of the firm. If the trade union is led by men who are opposed in principle to private enterprise, they may be ready to ruin the firm in order to

[1] G. D. H. Cole, *An Introduction to Social Theory* (London, 1920), p. 154.

force the government to nationalize it. A concerted attempt by all trade unions to obtain more pay than private industry can afford would be a method of securing its total nationalization independently of the ballot box in Parliamentary elections. On the other hand, it is possible to conceive of a free enterprise society in which employees paid fees to a specialized firm to bargain with employers on their behalf. Trade unions might become economically more effective if they developed into sorts of employment agency working for employees on a commission basis.

V

In practice, of course, trade unions have not been purely economic institutions. They have affiliations with medieval guilds of masters, workmen and apprentices, the members of which taught newcomers the skills of the trade, looked after the poorer members in sickness, paid burial expenses, and so on. Such bodies generally operated with a monopoly granted by the government, and were supposed to guarantee an adequate level of workmanship from their members. In England their function gradually became merely formal and convivial. In France they were abolished, three times over, it would seem, during the French Revolution. The most famous of these abolitions was the law of 14 June 1791, introduced by Le Chapelier, a physiocrat, who said: 'Undoubtedly it should be permitted to all citizens to assemble, but it should not be permitted to citizens of certain professions to assemble for their alleged common interests. There are no more guilds (*corporations*) in the state; there is nothing but the particular interest of each individual and the general interest. No one is permitted to inspire an intermediate interest in the citizens, to divide them from the public concern (*la chose publique*) by a guild spirit (*esprit de corporation*).' Le Chapelier went on to say that extreme poverty should be helped by the state, not by these self-interested guilds, and that it is for each individual to maintain the agreements he has made with his employer. No interest groups were to be allowed to come between the individual and the general will of the state.[1]

This point of view is stigmatized by Hegel in the *Phenomenology of Mind* when he writes of 'this undivided substance of absolute freedom' which 'elevates itself on to the throne of the world without there being

[1] See J. M. Thompson, *French Revolutionary Documents*. London, 1933. Earlier in 1791 the law of the Baron Leroy d'Allarde another physiocrat, abolished 'Jurandes', a type of corporation. Turgot had wanted to abolish these bodies, Marat, during the Revolution, to preserve them. Maurice Bouvier-Ajam, *Histoire du Travail en France*. Paris, 1957.

any power that can oppose it', and in which 'all classes and estates (Stände) which are the essence of mind, in which the whole is articulated, are erased.'[1] Those who, like Hegel, favour complex societies within which well-established social bodies maintain themselves and prevent the establishment of monolithic despotisms, may regard trade unions as sufficiently like guilds or corporations to justify their having analogous privileges. The maximum possible autonomy for trade unions may also be regarded as consistent with the view of government supported by Michael Oakeshott, according to which it is its function to keep the various groups, orders, classes and interests from upsetting the equilibrium or from maintaining it at an unfair level. Mr Harold Wilson seems to have adopted a variety of this view when he called for a 'social contract' between unions, employers and government to decide a general policy on wages, prices profits and growth.[2]

In fact, however, trade unions have been getting less and less like guilds. In the nineteenth century they acted as friendly societies, as educational bodies, as social clubs, as well as bargaining with employers on behalf of their members. One thing that Le Chapelier wanted has now happened – help for the poor is mostly provided by the state, so that the charitable functions of unions have largely been relinquished by them. Nor do they maintain many of their social functions, since entertainment is provided by many other organizations. What remains is their economic function, and this, as Oakeshott has pointed out, does not engage men's hearts in loyalty or friendship.[3]

It is true that the word 'solidarity' is much used in this connection, but it does not signify any close attachment to the union itself. This becomes apparent when we notice that in elections to office in some of the leading unions the total vote is ten per cent or less of the membership a figure which suggests that most members of these unions are no more morally attached to them than are shareholders to the companies in which they have invested. Those things have come to pass which G. D. H. Cole feared in his *Self-Government in Industry* (1917). Instead of local self-governing unions gaining influence within the firm, giant unions are bargaining with whole industries right across the country. The solidarity mentioned above shows itself not in the day-to-day work of the unions, since few members take part in this, nor in positive manifestations of mutual aid or companionship, but in a willingness to take part in strikes, or to continue loyal to them once they have been declared.

[1] In the subsection headed 'Absolute Freedom and Terror' in the section entitled 'Self-estranged Mind'.
[2] On 11 June, 1971.
[3] *Rationalism in Politics*, pp. 176–7.

VI

At the beginning of this paper I quoted from the fairly recently published *International Encyclopaedia of the Social Sciences* to the effect that in non-totalitarian countries strikes are no longer regarded as criminal but 'have, in degree, become institutionalized as one of the acknowledged sanctions of collective bargaining.' What other sanctions of collective bargaining there are is not clear from this, but perhaps the author had lock-outs in mind. As ordinarily understood, sanctions are penalties imposed by an authority to uphold a law, but strikes are not much like that. Wages are not established by law, and trade unions are not authorities entitled to enforce laws. They are parties in bargaining who prosecute their objectives with threats. This is rather different from ordinary bargaining where threats are not usual. If A and B are bargaining about potatoes, it is not generally possible for one party to say that the other party will not get any potatoes if he does not pay the price asked for. At any rate he can try elsewhere, but this is just what the employer cannot do when bargaining with a union. It will be said that the employer can threaten a lock-out, but the employer is prevented from selling his product (once stocks are exhausted) just as much by a lock-out as by a strike. The threats used in striking are no more sanctions than are the threats of monopolists, blackmailers or even bandits, who make acceptance of their demands more likely by presenting their victim with a disagreeable alternative.

But what I have said so far leaves out the disadvantages suffered by the individual who goes on strike. He loses financially, even when account is taken of public assistance (which lessens the burden on unions) and of the temporary jobs which strikers sometimes obtain. The longer the strike lasts the larger the increase necessary if the striker is to recoup his losses. Strikes are likely to bring losses to both parties and also to consumers of the firm's goods who, indeed, may lose more than either of the parties directly involved. Strikes are indeed a dismal device, and the term 'sanction' which I just now criticized, has at least the justification that all the parties to a strike are penalized, if only, some of them, for a time.

Sanctions, I suggest, should be contrasted with rewards. The main economic activities of firms and individuals are concerned with rewards or benefits. If A buys from B, A prefers the article he wants to buy to the money with which he buys it, B the money to the article, and both parties gain by the transaction. The manufacturer is out for profit, his customer for goods, whether for further profit or for enjoyment. But it is a different story when we come to employers and employees. They threaten one another with losses rather than offer gains. Is it in the nature of things that this should be so? Could employers and employees offer one another advantages instead of threatening one another with disadvantages?

At the end of section IV I suggested that trade unions ought to be transformed into a sort of employment agency. They would then become commercial firms, and those who had been members of unions would become individual clients having no permanent connection with the firm. I dwell on this idea, not because it has any prospect of being adopted, but in order to bring out the possibility of substituting the pursuit of advantages for the depressing threat of disadvantages that hangs over what are today called 'labour relations'. The threat, and therefore on occasion the exercise, of legal sanctions is essential to the state. Laws could not be upheld by offering rewards, for to whom could they be paid? To would-be breakers of the law? But if so, how could their law-breaking intentions be discovered before they were carried out? Would not everyone confess to such intentions in order to get the reward? Rewards go with commerce, sanctions with the state. Sanctions are required for the state to uphold the legal framework necessary for the honest conduct of business relations, and, historically and logically, replace coercion in the business sphere. If wage bargains are to be advantageous to both parties and to the community beyond them, both parties must wish for the success of the firm. Trade unions with no concern for the success of the firms in which their members work are revolutionary agencies.

In the Universal Declaration of Human Rights there is proclaimed a right to work, a right to equal pay for equal work, a right of the individual to form and join trade unions 'for the protection of his interests', but there is no mention of a right to strike. Perhaps this was omitted because representatives of Communist countries on the drafting committee were not willing to include a right that their governments had no intention of enforcing within their territories. Trade unionists express their adhesion to this 'right' when they describe going on strike as 'withdrawing labour'. But could it be claimed that an individual has a right to withdraw his labour altogether and be kept by the community for ever? Or that he has the right to cease working irrespective of any agreements he has made to work for a certain period? Withdrawing one's labour in the sense of ceasing to work for a particular firm is a very different thing from going on strike, which is participation in a collective act. Furthermore, it is a collective act designed to put others at a disadvantage, and it should be obvious that the amount and distribution of the disadvantage must be of concern to the state. One does not have to be a totalitarian to question the wisdom of including striking among the human rights.

Theatricality and Politics: Machiavelli's Concept of Fantasia

K. R. MINOGUE

January 1513 was the turning-point in Machiavelli's life. Behind him was a successful political and diplomatic career in the service of the Florentine Republic. This era of his life had ended with the somewhat inglorious flight of Soderini to Ragusa. What lay ahead was torture and danger of death, followed by the long, slow denouement of his life, in which he wrote the works that have made his name, whilst yet he pined for intimate involvement in the excitement of public affairs. During this abyss of his career, Machiavelli composed the rough draft of a letter in reply to one from Soderini. I propose to use the argument of this unpolished and very short composition[1] as a fulcrum on which to rest a view of Machiavelli's conception of political reality.

This procedure may require some defence. For, it might be objected, the best indication of a man's meaning comes from those writings over which he has laboured long in the effort to say precisely what he means. Rough work, by contrast, will often mislead because it will contain the purely mechanical implications of ill-considered sentences. In spite of this danger, however, the student of political writing will be wise to persevere with less finished work, for what he often wants to know is – what is the writer *not* interested in telling him. Occasionally, it is even a case of seeking for beliefs which the writer holds, but would prefer not to make explicit.

Now in the case of Machiavelli, we have to deal with a writer of matchless austerity, one preoccupied to the exclusion of almost all else with a single concern: to create a technique of political success. Machiavelli

[1] The letter is numbered 119 in Vol. VI (*Lettre*) of the *Opere Complete* published in Milan by Feltrinelli. In the widely accessible *Letters of Machiavelli* edited by Allan Gilbert (New York 1961) it is numbered 116. Roberto Ridolfi criticizes Villari for having overlooked 'this most important letter'. (The Life of *Niccolo Machiavelli* (London, 1963), translated from the Italian edition of 1954, ch. 13, n.6.)

teases his reader by the way in which his path takes him near to philosophical considerations, personal relevation, insights into the spiritual condition of his life, or the features of all human skill; and yet, he hardly ever diverges from his chosen objective. This is one of the reasons why Machiavelli is thought to be a great and suggestive political thinker, and yet, simultaneously, disappointingly banal.[1] In spite of the fact that his happiest moments were spent in intimate involvement with concrete and particular historical events, Machiavelli is one of the most timeless of all political writers. For in all his work we find the simplicity of a distilled concern for what a certain type of European has regarded as fundamental, irrespective of whether we are concerned with the Greeks or the modern European. Such a writer has no interest in revealing to us so speculative a matter as the general psychology with which he works, any more than an actress is interested in the chemistry of greasepaint. It is only in moments of great stress that such matters will achieve a fleeting sharpness of focus.

Let us turn to the letter. It has a central concern which is familiar from later writings, and since Machiavelli's mind works by way of the suggestive example, we may call it the Hannibal–Scipio problem: 'Hannibal and Scipio, besides their military attainments, in which the two excelled equally, one of them with cruelty, treachery, and lack of religion kept his armies united in Italy and made himself admired by the people, who to follow him rebelled against the Romans; the other chieved the same result in Spain with mercy, loyalty and piety; both of them won countless victories'.

How is it, Machiavelli wonders, that two diametrically opposed policies both lead to success? Typically, he proceeds to explore the problem with examples: Lorenzo de' Medici disarmed the people to hold Florence, Giovanni Bentivoglio armed them to hold Bologna, both succeeded. Some have succeeded by building fortresses to hold their territory, others by destroying them. In a marginal note, Machiavelli sharpens the antithesis by observing that 'it is not possible to have fortresses and not to have them, to be both cruel and compassionate'. He remembers the Emperor Titus who 'believed that he would lose his position on any day when he did not benefit somebody' and adds that there is no doubt a contrary case. Since this is merely a draft, he can't think of one, and no doubt confessions of malevolence are harder to find than professions of benevolence. What he needs is a real personage resembling the villainous Moor, Aaron, in *Titus Andronicus*, who remarks as he is led away to his death:

[1] e.g. Irving Kristol, 'Machiavelli', *Encounter*, December 1954, p. 49; Sydney Anglo: *Machiavelli: A Dissection*. London 1969.

THE MORALITY OF POLITICS

> If one good deed in all my life I did,
> I do repent it from my very soul.

Such is the problem; and there is no doubt why it is a problem for Machiavelli. If there is no solution to it beyond the cliché that circumstances alter cases, then there is little hope for the construction of a technique of political success. The point of the technique is power, the method is economy. When, later in the year, Machiavelli offered his famous gift to Lorenzo, what he claimed for it was the power 'of enabling you to understand in a very short time all those things which I have learnt at the cost of privation and danger in the course of many years'. This was, of course, a Renaissance project, and its method was elaborated a century later by Bacon; but it accorded very well with Machiavelli's own temperament. 'You want to know in two hours what I have not been able to find out in many months' remarked an ambassador of the Duke of Savoy who had been subject for an evening to Machiavelli's insatiable curiosity.[1]

The general principles of Machiavelli's technique, then, would offer mankind escape from the frustrating condition of acquiring knowledge (that is, power) *only* from experience. It would allow of easy transmission and of growth. What had been learned could be formulated as a set of applicable maxims. But the economy of these maxims depended upon abstraction; and this meant that every increase of economy brought with it a corresponding diminution of specificity. The problem, stated in this form, is a perfectly general one in the logic of practical reason. Any set of practical maxims governing an activity will require a further set of general statements, referring both to circumstances and to the existing maxims, to indicate which of two contradictories is appropriate to the case in hand. But then, the regulative principles at this higher level are themselves also equivocal, and call therefore for a further set at a higher level to determine which of them shall be applied. And so on, in a regress which cannot be stopped.

This is a statement in logical terms of the more casual truth that a human activity requires, in addition even to the most exhaustive equipment of maxims, some element of human judgement which cannot be resolved into principles. Stated in this latter form, the point appears intuitionist, and has an air of dogmatism about it; but as a point of the logic of practical reason, it is unassailable. Certainly Machiavelli was perfectly familiar with the difficulty, and this letter is in part a response to it.

To state the matter in these terms is, however, an anachronism, for Machiavelli certainly never thought in terms of logical regresses, or,

[1] Quoted Ridolfi, op. cit., p. 101.

THEATRICALITY AND POLITICS

in any serious way, in terms of practical reason. What he actually did was to invoke *Fortuna* as a formal solution to the problem. It is certainly true, he writes, that 'anybody wise enough to understand the times and the types of affairs and to adapt himself to them would have always good fortune, or he would protect himself always from bad, and it would come to be true that the wise man would rule the stars and the Fates. But because there never are such wise men, since men in the first place are short-sighted, and in the second cannot command their natures, it follows that Fortune varies and commands men and holds them under her yoke'. Bad fortune, in other words, is always the consequence of human error, and a god-like invulnerability is at least conceivable.

But in later writings, Machiavelli abandons this view, and incorporates in the concept of Fortuna all those many contingencies, many of them logically beyond any possible human competence, with which men must live. Here then is a distinction between what Machiavelli sought to argue, and what – a few months later – he thought it possible to believe. The famous passage in the *Prince* in which he recognizes Fortuna as the determinant of half, or perhaps a little more, of human destiny, represents his extremely rapid change of mind.

These considerations, then, appear to dominate the letter, and on a superficial reading, it would seem merely to anticipate the fuller discussion in the *Discourses*, III, Chapters 9, 21 and 22. What makes the letter vastly more significant, however, is the presence of a line of argument which can be indicated by four statements which find a place in, as it were, the interstices of the letter. Two of them, it is important to note, are marginal comments on the draft – a point which could not be gathered from Allan Gilbert's translation. The statements I am concerned with are the following, and I have used Gilbert's translation:

Ciascuno secondo la sua fantasia si governa.
Each man according to his own imagination guides himself.

La famiglia, la città, ognuno ha la fortuna sua fondata sul modo del procedere suo, et ciascuna di loro si stracca, et quando la é stracca bisogna racquistarla con uno altro modo.
The family, the city, every man has his Fortune founded on his way of proceeding, and each Fortune tires, and when she is tired, she must be got back in another way.

... ciascuno secondo lo ingegno et fantasia sua si governa.
each man conducts himself according to his disposition and his imagination.

Ma perché i tempi et le cose universalmente et particularmente si mutano spesso, et gli huomini non mutano le loro fantasie né i loro modi di procedere, accade che uno ha un tempo buona fortuna, et un tempo trista.

Thus, because times and affairs in general and individually change often, and men do not change their imaginings and their procedures, it happens that a man at one time has good fortune and at another time bad.

Here then is an idea which keeps bubbling to the surface of Machiavelli's thought. It is most often indicated by the term *fantasia*, which Gilbert translates as 'imagination', but whilst we may use the term *fantasia* as the name of the idea, we must not fall into the vulgar notion that the idea is only present when the word is being used. For in the course of this letter alone, we shall find four terms being used almost synonymously to deal with the same complex thought: 'disposition', 'manner of proceeding', 'nature', and 'imagination' itself – all of them are ways of specifying the mental organization that determines behaviour. And in the course of this letter, stimulated no doubt by catastrophe, Machiavelli is preoccupied by a vision of politics as an encounter of these things, summed up (in this letter, though not in later writings) as the outcome of *Fortuna*. Politics is an encounter of private worlds such

> That, if it would but apprehend some joy,
> It comprehends some bringer of that joy;
> Or in the night, imagining some fear,
> How easy is a bush suppos'd a bear!

Our business, then, is to explore Machiavelli's theory of imagination.

The theory is essentially sceptical, although Machiavelli's entirely conventional acceptance of many common-sense distinctions obscures the point. '... the great majority of mankind', we read in *Discourses* I Chapter 25, 'are satisfied with appearances, as though they were realities, and are often even more influenced by the things that seem than by those that are'. This does indeed sound like the common-sense view that all that glisters is not gold – implying that there really *is* gold. But where is this 'gold' to be found? It consists simply in how things seem to other men – along, perhaps, with any general understanding we may acquire of how these 'seemings' may change. Machiavelli's concept of imagination is in part the doctrine that political reality is constituted of nothing else but 'seemings'. It is of course true that I may falsely believe a man to be my friend who is 'really' my enemy: but that reality is only an unstable part of a flux in which everything is dissolved into appearance by being continually construed as the product of imagination.

The significance of this element of Machiavelli's thought has been clearly related to the tradition of political philosophy in an excellent

[1] *Prince*, Chapter XXV.

discussion by Sheldon Wolin: 'Machiavelli's approach to this matter, his conception of political nature, can best be understood by way of a question suggested by Plato: what would be the consequences for political thought and action if man's condition were that of permanent resident in the Cave?'[1] What we have to deal with is a consistent and thoroughgoing scepticism, even though the range and consistency of the position have been obscured by a misleadingly conventional terminology. In terms of common sense, we live in a shared world, and any differences of judgement may be regarded as varying 'interpretations' of this common reality. The technique of the sceptic is to demolish the common-ness of this world on the ground that it is no more than an unstable and temporary inference from what is, for the moment, common to individual understandings. The attention of the philosophical sceptic is consistently directed away from what is said about the world towards the psychology of saying anything about it at all. Machiavelli's concept of *fantasia* is, then, a typical sceptic's device, but its importance is almost wholly obscured by the fact that Machiavelli is content, in virtually all his published writings, to take it for granted.

One area in which the theory may be seen at work is when Machiavelli deals with *necessita*: 'men never endure inconveniences unless some powerful necessity compels them', he writes in a typical passage in the *History of Florence*.[2] Politics is in part the engineering of necessity: sometimes to create situations where men have no alternative, as when generals are advised to position their troops in such a way that the only alternative to victory is death; and sometimes to prevent the occurrence of a necessity, as when Machiavelli cautions against putting men in a position where they seem to have no alternative but to kill or be killed.[3] Now *necessita* is always a matter of imagination. For although it is easy, in reading Machiavelli's mature writings, to imagine that *necessita* qualifies a real situation, imagination is always a mediate term. For we are always dealing with a state of mind, or structure of the imagination, which takes for granted the extremely common, though not universal, aversion to death.

But just as it is characteristic of imagination on some occasions to obliterate the human perception of alternatives, resulting in *necessita*, so also it may operate to show men alternatives they might not otherwise realize. '. . . knowing afar off (which it is only given to a prudent man

[1] *Politics and Vision* (London 1960), p. 211.
[2] II, 1.
[3] The story of Queen Rosamund in the *History of Florence* I, 2, illustrates the ubiquity of the principle. For Rosamund, acting upon strictly Machiavellian principles, seduced a Lombard noble in order to offer him the alternative of being executed for his presumption – or killing the King. He made the latter choice.

to do) the evils that are brewing, they are easily cured,' he tells the Prince in Chapter III. The prudence which is in most writers attributed to rationality appears in Machiavelli as a function of the energy of imagination. Here, as in many respects, Hobbes may be seen as philosophically reformulating much that Machiavelli puts in a more casual manner. Hobbes takes prudence to be 'much memory'; it is a stock of situations experienced which may be used in understanding the future. The fact of having experienced them in the past makes it easier to imagine them in the future. Imagination thus comes down, in the end, to thinkability, and men's imaginations differ primarily in what they believe to be thinkable. Thus Machiavelli observes that the Prince who has lost a territory and then reconquered it is in a stronger position, 'for the ruler is now, by the fact of the rebellion, less averse to secure his position by punishing offenders, unmasking suspects, and strengthening himself in weak places'.[1]

From what we have so far said, it might appear that Machiavelli equates success in politics with range of imagination. The man to whom anything is thinkable has, in certain respects, resources not available to those of less imagination. Thus Hannibal's success – part of his *virtu* – is that he can commit cruelties which other men might regard as out of the question. Clearly it is the case that the figures whom Machiavelli most admires are distinguished by an imaginative range beyond the stale and repetitive imaginings of the ordinary run of men. Yet in many of the most interesting cases, precisely the reverse is the case; and this appears most clearly if we consider Machiavelli's view of religion.

Machiavelli regards religion as 'the most necessary and assured support of any civil society'.[2] His interest in the matter begins and ends, as everybody knows, with the effects upon political behaviour of any religious belief. There can be no more explicit statement of his view that reality is essentially political than his account of the religion of the Romans; 'Nor had this system of consulting the auspices any other object than to inspire the soldiers on the eve of battle with that confidence which is the surest guaranty of victory.'[3] Moses, who transmitted laws from God, and Numa 'who feigned that he held converse with a nymph, who dictated to him all that he wished to persuade the people to' are all one on this scale of interpretation. Simple uncivilized men are most receptive of religious beliefs, but it is not impossible to influence thoroughly civilized men in just the same way; and on this point Machiavelli cites Savonarola, who persuaded 'an immense number' of Florentines that he held converse with God. Machiavelli explicitly

[1] *Prince*, III.
[2] *Discourses*, I, Chapter 11.
[3] *Discourses*, I, 14.

disclaims any concern with the truth of this claim, and goes on to attribute its successful propagation to 'the purity of his life, the doctrines he preached, and the subjects he selected for his discourses.'[1]

Politics, then, may be represented in Machiavellian terms as the engineering of imagination. It consists of persuading men to think certain things, and to recognize certain limits of what is thinkable. The precision of these limits is constantly eroding; a long period of peace facilitates some beliefs, and renders others more difficult of acceptance. A country long at peace begins to take its security for granted; one that is frequently at war will make better provision. The periodic occurrence of salutary acts of terror in the name of the state is a manner of sustaining a constant and vital public imagination. Such acts, we learn in the first chapter of the Third Book of the *Discourses* (which is the definitive statement of this position) ought to take place no less frequently than every ten years. Sometimes, Machiavelli is happy to observe, Fortune herself supplies the occasion of a reaffirmation of necessity in the form of external attack. The Romans had the inestimable benefit of an attack by the Gauls, which caused them to return to their original principles. But any sound constitution regulating the political activities of a virtuous people will make provision for such constancy.

The assumption which underlies this argument is that of a *natural* movement towards laxity and decay. After a period of peace, that is to say, men begin to imagine that it is no longer necessary to persevere with military exercises and the other rigours and niceties which were originally established by a wise lawgiver in response to civic necessity. New pleasures become thinkable as the imagination plays with what is possible. These laxities, the development of private imaginations in place of a unified and disciplined public imagination, are precisely what Machiavelli means by corruption; and the business of religion and of political skill is, jointly, to prevent it from happening. And, since our interpretation of Machiavelli is one which serves to stress his similarity with Hobbes, we may note that both men believe that a simple paradox is at the root of political wisdom: out of good comes evil, and out of evil good.

For the point of political skill is to maintain a strong, secure and peaceful state; and maintaining such a state creates the condition of internal and civil disturbance. But civil disturbance, or military weakness, which are themselves evils, are prone to create the political necessities which will call up the resolution for regeneration. Machiavelli's sense of cyclicity is no doubt Polybian; and when we read (to take a typical formulation from the *History of Florence*) that: 'valour produces peace; peace repose; repose disorder, disorder, ruin; so from

[1] *Discourses*, I, 11.

disorder order springs; from order virtue, and from this, glory and good fortune',[1] then we should be mistaken if the Polybian echo prevented us from recognizing the distinctively Machiavellian psychology involved. Hobbes, of course, believes that a philosopher can rationally demonstrate the state as a necessity; but for the great mass of men, the only teacher of political wisdom is the experience of the state of nature, which moulds their imagining of what is possible or impossible.

Politics is, then, in a deep sense, an exercise in theatricality. And the perception that this is the case has nothing whatever to do with the fact that Machiavelli is a dramatist. *Mandragola* casts remarkably little light on his politics. But his account of political skill is primarily an account of how to play upon the passions of an audience, the first condition of whose existence is that their attention must primarily be focused upon the stage of public affairs.

In the letter to Soderini, we find Machiavelli remarking: 'I see, not with your mirror, where nothing is seen but prudence, but with that of the many, which is obliged in affairs to judge the result when they are finished, and not the means while they are going on.' This is an obscure utterance – it is the passage glossed by the first of those remarks about fantasia which we have already quoted – but what it seems to involve (along with a certain irony at Soderini's expense) is a distinction in politics between the participants and the audience, and this seems to be the underlying image wherever Machiavelli seems to be talking about an élite. In terms of this image, a healthy state is one where the play has caught and dominated the emotions of the audience, whilst corruption, which preoccupies Machiavelli as much as *virtu*, is simply a boring play which has failed to capture the imagination, with the result that the audience falls to muttering and quarrelling, the actors being left talking to themselves and it is with politics, as with audiences, that men do have a constant natural tendency to be distracted unless their attention has been caught and held. It is not merely Fortuna which is fickle and feminine; or, rather, part of the reason *why* Fortuna is thus capricious, is that her operations depend upon the behaviour of large numbers of unstable and easily swayed masses. The primary political realities that Machiavelli recognizes are, then, generalities – which can only be formal – about the working of imagination.

The first and most important of these generalities is the one we have just been discussing: the fact that there is no fixity at all in the workings of *fantasia*, and any required fixity must be supplied by carefully engineered events. Proneness to boredom is the first law of politics, something which Machiavelli had already recognized, though (he affirms to Soderini) only tentatively, in the letter we have earlier con-

[1] Book V, Chapter 1.

sidered. 'Cruelty, treachery and irreligion are enough to give reputation to a new ruler in a province where humanity, loyalty and religion have been common practice for a long time, while humanity, loyalty and religion are sufficient where cruelty, treachery and irreligion have dominated for a time, because, as bitter things disturb the taste and sweet ones cloy it, so men get bored with good and complain of ill.'

This is the way Machiavelli solves the puzzle of Hannibal and Scipio. And the really striking point about Machiavelli's putting it at the centre of his understanding of politics is that it is something that a rationalist thinker of politics would have to explain away. It is a principle which dashes the hopes of all believers, all ideologists, and all who seek to enshrine, amongst the flux of human affairs, some value which is permanent and permanently available to men.

It is an indication of the subtlety of his position that the same letter contains a further principle of the imagination which appears, on the face of it, to be the exact contradictory of what we have just been discussing: 'because times and affairs in general and individually change often, and men do not change their imagining and their procedures, it happens that a man at one time has good fortune and at another bad.' And in another place,[1] Machiavelli remarks that men find it hard to imagine that what has brought them success in the past will not go on doing so.

The imagination, then, is subject to a certain hardening and rigidity which is analogous to the natural processes of the body, but which can be explained in psychological terms. This is a principle of wide generality and great currency. Arnold Toynbee, we may remember, has used it to explain the fall of civilizations. Yet, as we have seen, this principle appears to contradict Machiavelli's equally firm insistence upon the instability of men's imagining: he appears to be suggesting that the imagination both is, and is not, stable. The solution to this difficulty derives from the fact that Machiavelli believes that *our own* imaginings tend towards repetition, whilst our responses to how other men act (which derives from *their* imagination) is radically unstable. The apparently contradictory principles have different areas of operation.

It would carry us much beyond the range of this argument to show the full ramifications of Machiavelli's constant awareness that political actions derive directly from the character of a man's imagination. It will suffice to do two things. Firstly, to illustrate a little further how this understanding is used, and secondly to consider what light our attending to this concept may throw upon some of the more persistent questions of Machiavellian discussion.

Machiavelli never for a moment loses sight of the fact that a political

[1] *Discourses*, III, 9. cf. *Prince*, Chapter XXV.

circumstance is never an unequivocal happening in the world, but that what it *is* depends upon its reflection in the mind of a participant: 'Men', he typically says,[1] 'neither know how to be entirely good nor wholly bad; and it so happens almost invariably that a general, after a great victory, is unwilling to leave his army, and to conduct himself with becoming modesty, and knows not how to take a decided course, which has in itself something honourable and grand; and thus he remains undecided, and whilst in this ambiguous state he is crushed.' Men are, that is to say, victimized by their imaginations.

If we press very hard upon passages such as these, we may extract a doctrine to the effect that it is a man's imagination which determines what knowledge he has and what abilities he may use. Imagination is the guide and governor of an individual's manifold potentialities. It not uncommonly leads men into dangerous acts: 'a man who has a guilty conscience readily thinks that everybody is speaking of him. You may overhear a word spoken to someone else that will greatly disturb you, because you think it has reference to you, and may cause you either to discover the conspiracy by flight, or embarrass its execution by hastening it before the appointed time.'[2] The conspirator, rather like the general who is endangered by his great victory, is suffering from what one might call an 'inflammation' of the imagination: what seemed unthinkable before has now become a temptation. And what makes this new stage of *fantasia* more than mere fantasy is the fact that a corresponding change has taken place in the attitudes to him of his soldiers and of the population at large. And the ruler of a state in which such changes have taken place must now face a new situation, one which arises simply from a restructuring of imagination.

By recognizing this preoccupation in Machiavelli, we save ourselves from making quite simple mistakes of identification. Machiavellianism in politics, since it derives from a scepticism about the ideals and beliefs held by political men, might seem to be identifiable with cynicism. We might, thinking along these lines, expect Machiavelli to be most impressed by the credulity of mankind, and we might support this view by referring to his treatment of auguries and soothsayers in the first Book of the *Discourses*. This plausible interpretation would, however, be singularly wrong. For it is not the human capacity for being taken in which impresses Machiavelli so much as its opposite: the way in which men's imaginations settle feebly upon what little experience they have had. 'It is a common fault of men not to reckon on storms in fair weather,' he tells us in Chapter XIV of the *Prince*, a chapter preliminary to his fuller discussion of Fortune as an impetuous, turbulent – and

[1] *Discourses*, I, Chapter 30.
[2] *Discourses*, III, Chapter 6.

unexpected – river. And much earlier, in Chapter VI, when discussing the difficulties facing the man who tries to create a new political structure, he notes among the difficulties not only the fact that some have profited by the old order and that the supporters of the new are likely to be lukewarm, but also 'the incredulity of mankind, who do not truly believe in anything new until they have had actual experience of it.' Empiricism, in Machiavelli's view, is the seedbox of mediocrity.

'Since Machiavelli,' runs a typical judgement on Machiavelli's significance in the history of European thought, 'a dimension has been amputated from man's political consciousness.'[1] Most writers on Machiavelli sooner or later begin to strike this rather alarming key. And, like Kristol, they all suggest that something valuable has been lost. For it is clear that Machiavelli describes for us a politics in which any consistent allegiance to humanity, justice, mercy, loyalty and fidelity has been abandoned. To put the matter another way, Machiavelli accords to the political practitioner a much greater freedom from moral restraint than any other significant theorist. It is hard for the reader not to regard this freedom as a Greek gift, and its actualization as the loss of what was once valuable shelter and protection. Our next concern must be to sketch the argument by which Machiavelli reaches this conclusion, and to consider the place of the concept of *fantasia* in it.

Politics is, by general agreement, an area of hope and fear. It contains nothing which does not elicit from us some version of these key emotions. They are, indeed, so powerful that they have left their mark, not only on political activity itself, but also upon nearly all attempts to describe and explain what the activity is about. Political theory at all levels, that is to say, has been marked by the intrusion of desirabilities and unthinkabilities whose presence testifies not to analytical perception but to the hopes and fears of the theorist himself. These desirabilities are supported by reasons. Hence the underlying desirability on whose centrality a great number of theorists have all agreed is Reason itself. And Reason has set limits to political freedom by circumscribing imagination.

A great deal of the most influential political thinking from Greek times to modern has been of this constrictive character. On Machiavelli's view of the matter, this kind of thinking is the equivalent of identifying drama itself with tragedy, or with social criticism, or the proscenium arch, or the three unities, or some other currently admired manner of constructing plays. The great fault of political theory, then, has been parochiality disguised as metaphysics, the weakness for believing that local rules and preferences are part of reality itself.

Some writers have, indeed, avoided this Platonic error, and argued

[1] Irving Kristol, op. cit., p. 52.

against construing Reason as the essence of politics. They have therefore purged their account of politics of any norms or allegiance thought to rest upon some rational basis. But they have not been able to take the final step of purging their account of politics of any element of belief at all. They have taken the view that politics depends upon *some* agreement, even though they have recognized that the actual content of the belief will be some contingent result of local preference. But *any* belief has a logic, and that logic may in time become a construction and a limitation upon the political imagination. What looks at first like a satisfactory recognition of the true instability of our position turns out to contain limiting elements.

Now in Machiavelli's treatment of politics, all such limitations have been dispensed with in the only way possible: they have been ignored. To have argued against them would constitute a covert allegiance to something which had to be superseded. The full significance of the concept of *fantasia* is that it replaces reason in a more conventional political thinking. Political activity is thus not the copying of some rational order, nor is it the establishment of an agreed belief on the ends of public order. It is simply a constantly changing concordance of the public imagination, and the business of politics is to maintain that concordance by any means available. For whilst reason is public, ordered, and predictable, *fantasia* (by which, as we have seen, men guide themselves) is private, chaotic and unstable. Disagreements over what is desirable do at least belong to the one world; they may logically be brought into relation with one another; diverse imaginings hardly belong to the same world at all.

Disagreement is potentially manageable by argument: incomprehension is not. It can be dealt with only by distraction, diversion, occasionally argument, and frequently by force. But unless the potential incomprehension of the human situation is dealt with by vigorous political creativity, then the consequence will be the miseries of a corrupt society – and mankind is such that the very success of politics in creating a stable community provides the conditions of its own decay. This observation of cyclicity in Machiavelli was to be philosophically elaborated by Hobbes.

History is in these terms the unstable realm which the human imagination manages to snatch from the imaginative poverty to which human beings naturally tend. Seen from these austere heights, both the making and the destroying of empires, the lunatic aspirations of a Charles XII or a Hitler, the self-immolating passions of religious wars, the philanthropic and managerial passions of modern times – all of these things are no more than the ceaseless play of human political imaginings, each temporary and doomed to supersession, and each constituting a framework within which rational desirabilities (along with every other civilized activity) may find a place. The true politician is the one who uses the imaginings of men to keep the activity going; the politician who succumbs to any of the temporary desirabilities thrown up by politics has abandoned his vocation: he has become the material of politics rather than its practitioner.

There is, of course, a problem here, and one which the framework of this article cannot accommodate. How is it possible for politicians who, like other men, are guided according to their own *fantasia*, to stand above the imaginings of others? The answer must be that this is a difficult and intermittent achievement, and that Machiavelli's use of the term *virtu* is partly designed to describe it. But it is certainly true that most politicians who sense themselves moving towards destruction because of allegiance to some local desirability will take rapid steps to disencumber themselves of it well before the point of disaster. Men, of course, living in the plain commonly judge politicians according to their loyalty; but they do so, Machiavelli believes, only because they do not understand the true character of politics.

Machiavelli's scepticism is, then, all the more complete precisely because he never bothers to argue it. Argument has always been the sceptic's weakness, his concession to an activity whose validity would destroy his case. It is not, of course, that Machiavelli does not have beliefs. His view is that everything in the way of civilization is based upon the establishment of the state[1] and that that establishment, the condition of rationality as it is the condition of everything else in culture, is itself a kind of irrationality.

To say that Machiavelli separated ethics from politics – a weaker version of Kristal's amputation metaphor – does not go far enough. For the point of Christian ethics, indeed of any ethics that begin with the private will, is to supply criteria regulating (and thus limiting) politics. But Machiavelli believed, not that moral aims were the condition of politics, but rather that politics – the activity of sustaining a communal life, indeed a communal imagination – was the condition without which the ethical aims from time to time embraced by men could not come into existence. The creative imagination of a Romulus or a Moses, with its inevitable accompaniment of violence (than which few things more vigorously affect the imagination) is the necessary preliminary to all moral life.

Paradoxically, might makes right – not in the sense that the mighty have a right to do what they do, but in the sense that until some might has established a state, there is no soil in which the plant of morality, as it may locally be conceived, may grow. What Machiavelli most hates

[1] *Discourses*, I, Chapter 2.

about the Christian religion is its powerful tendency to kill its own sustaining medium: as if the plant should destroy the soil.

The argument of this paper, then, is that in discussions of Machiavelli, too much attention has been paid to explicit concepts such as *virtú*, *fortuna* and *necessita*, and not enough to those less prominent ideas which constitute, as it were, the medium within which Machiavelli conceives of politics. In particular, the idea of *fantasia* is important because it is the vehicle of Machiavelli's scepticism, and it is this concealed scepticism which gives his readers the impression that he has revealed an abyss in the human situation, amputated dimensions of consciousness and similar, appropriately melodramatic, metaphors.

Fantasia functions as Machiavelli's almost entirely implicit alternative to reason in traditional political thinking. To recognize it as such has the great advantage of allowing us to understand politics a good deal more purely, that is, less encumbered with local pieties, than would otherwise be the case. But perhaps even more than that, to recognize political ideals and aspirations as inhabitants of a world of *fantasia* is to abandon the illusory security of moral absolutes, addiction to which so commonly closes the mind.

INDEX

Anderson, P., 76n.
Anglo, S., 115n., 149n.
Anscombe, G. E. M., 27, 93n.
Aquinas, T., 83
Arendt, H., 73n., 108n.
Aristotle, 49n., 60, 83, 119

Bacon, F., 150
Baier, K., 92n., 97
Baker, A. J., 125n.
Barry, B., 43n.
Bentham, J., 83
Bentley, A. F., 118
Bergson, H., 26
Bernstein, E., 76n., 77n., 78
Blackburn, R., 76n.
Bouvier-Ajam, M., 144n.
Briggs, A., 79n.
Brogan, D., 103n.
Bull, H., 101
Burke, E., 136
Burnham, J., 114, 117–19, 123, 126–7, 131, 133
Butterfield, H., 53n., 111, 117n., 120

Chabod, F., 115
Cole, G. D. H., 143, 145
Collingwood, R. G., 123
Crick, B., 31–4, 39, 45, 46, 49–50
Croce, B., 115

Djilas, M., 79n.

Dray, W., 123n.

Engels, F., 104

Fanon, F., 88n.
Finer, S. E., 125, 127n., 128n., 132, 135
Fitch, J. A., 137
Florence, P. S., 114n.
Forsyth, M. G., 101n.
Frankena, W. F., 94n.

Galbraith, J. K., 95n.
Gay, P., 76n.
Gerth, H. H., 66n., 127n.
Gierke, O., 136
Gilbert, A., 148n., 151, 152
Ginsberg, M., 37n.

Hare, R. M., 67n., 91–4
Hart, H. L. A., 96
Hegel, G. W. F., 110, 144, 145
Hobbes, T., 52, 110, 154, 155, 160
Hoffman, S. H., 111n.
Hook, S., 76n.
Hume, D., 121
Huxley, A., 71n.

Jensen, De L., 52n.
Jouvenel, B. de 31–3, 49

Kant, J., 26, 27, 29, 91, 101n.
Kautsky, K., 78

163

INDEX

Keens-Soper, A., 101n.
Kristol, I., 149n., 159n., 161

Laslett, P., 11
Lenin, V. I., 48, 104
Lerner, M., 52, 55
Leroy d'Allarde, P., 144n.
Locke, J., 83

Machiavelli, N., 52–5, 60–1, 110, 115–17, 119, 120, 122, 126–8, 131, 133–4, 148ff.
Maistre, J. de, 78
Maitland, F. W., 136
Mao Tse-Tung, 28, 105, 107
Marx, K., 9, 104, 127, 131, 141
Mattingley, G., 110n.
Meinecke, F., 115, 116, 123n.
Meisel, J., 134n.
Michels, R., 117, 122, 126, 128, 133, 134
Mill, J. S., 82n.
Mills, C. W., 66n., 127n.
Milne, A. J. M., 136n.
Mitrany, D., 111n.
Moore, G. E., 97
Morgenthau, H., 111n., 112n.
Mosca, G., 117, 119–22, 124, 126, 128, 132n., 133, 134

Niebuhr, R., 112

Oakeshott, M., 145
O'Brien, C. C., 75n., 107

Pareto, V., 117, 119–26, 128–32, 134
Plamenatz, J. P., 11
Plato, 9, 21, 56, 59, 60, 153
Plumb, J. H., 110n.
Pollock, F., 116n.
Popper, Sir Karl, 124

Quinton, A., 43n.

Raphael, D. D., 126
Ridolphi, R., 148n., 150n.
Rousseau, J-J., 115
Runciman, W. G., 11
Russell, B., 67n.
Ryan, A., 123n.

Sartre, J-P., 27, 66
Savigear, P., 101n.
Shaw, G. B., 79n.
Shelvankar, K. S., 71n.
Socrates, 59
Sorel, G., 117
Stalin, I. V., 78
Strauss, L., 115, 127n.
Strawson, P. F., 92n., 95n.
Stretton, H., 126n.

Taylor, A. J. P., 104
Thompson, J. M., 144n.
Thompson, K. W., 112n.
Tönnies, F., 101
Toynbee, A., 157
Trotzky, L. D., 78
Truman, D., 118

Vanech, W. D., 75n.
Vico, G., 25
Villari, P., 148n.
Voegelin, E., 111n., 113n.

Walker, A. D. M., 92n.
Walker, L. J., 120n.
Wallace, G., 92n.
Warnock, G. J., 11
Webb, S., 19n.
Weber, M., 66n., 67n., 76
Wight, M., 109
Winch, P., 123, 125
Wolin, S. S., 152

For Product Safety Concerns and Information please contact our EU representative GPSR@taylorandfrancis.com
Taylor & Francis Verlag GmbH, Kaufingerstraße 24, 80331 München, Germany

www.ingramcontent.com/pod-product-compliance
Lightning Source LLC
Chambersburg PA
CBHW052128300426
44116CB00010B/1820